Strategies for Developing and Supporting School Leaders

Strategies for Developing and Supporting School Leaders assists personnel in school districts to deliver appropriate development and support practices for aspiring and current school leaders. This book explores a variety of research-based and best-practice processes that can be implemented in school districts to prepare leaders to meet the technical and adaptive demands of school leadership and the needs of a diverse student population.

Sanzo lays out a cohesive framework of key processes and activities that range from the very simple and immediately implementable to the more complex and nuanced. Providing both the "how" and "why," this important resource shares ideas, strategies, tools, and systems to develop effective and meaningful professional learning opportunities to help promote highly effective schools and districts.

Karen L. Sanzo is Associate Professor and Program Coordinator of the Educational Leadership Program at Old Dominion University, USA. She is also the Director of the School Leadership Preparation and Development Network and assists Virginia schools and districts with leadership preparation development and formative assessment leadership.

Other Eye On Education Books Available from Routledge
(www.routledge.com/eyeoneducation)

Formative Assessment Leadership: Identify, Plan, Apply, Assess, Refine
Karen L. Sanzo, Steve Myran, and John Caggiano

The Leader's Guide to Working with Underperforming Teachers: Overcoming Marginal Teaching and Getting Results
Sally Zepeda

Five Critical Leadership Practices: The Secret to High-Performing Schools
Ruth C. Ash and Pat H. Hodge

Mentoring Is a Verb: Strategies for Improving College and Career Readiness
Russ Olwell

How to Make Data Work: A Guide for Educational Leaders
Jenny Grant Rankin

Hiring the Best Staff for Your School: How to Use Narrative to Improve Your Recruiting Process
Rick Jetter

What Connected Educators Do Differently
Todd Whitaker, Jeffrey Zoul, and Jimmy Casas

BRAVO Principal! Building Relationships with Actions that Value Others, 2nd Edition
Sandra Harris

Job-Embedded Professional Development: Support, Collaboration, and Learning in Schools
Sally J. Zepeda

Get Organized! Time Management for School Leaders, 2nd Edition
Frank Buck

The Educator's Guide to Writing a Book: Practical Advice for Teachers and Leaders
Cathie E. West

Strategies for Developing and Supporting School Leaders

Stepping Stones to Great Leadership

Karen L. Sanzo

Routledge
Taylor & Francis Group
NEW YORK AND LONDON

First published 2016
by Routledge
711 Third Avenue, New York, NY 10017

and by Routledge
2 Park Square, Milton Park, Abingdon, Oxon, OX14 4RN

Routledge is an imprint of the Taylor & Francis Group, an informa business

© 2016 Taylor & Francis

The right of Karen L. Sanzo to be identified as author of this work has been asserted by her in accordance with sections 77 and 78 of the Copyright, Designs and Patents Act 1988.

All rights reserved. No part of this book may be reprinted or reproduced or utilised in any form or by any electronic, mechanical, or other means, now known or hereafter invented, including photocopying and recording, or in any information storage or retrieval system, without permission in writing from the publishers.

Trademark notice: Product or corporate names may be trademarks or registered trademarks, and are used only for identification and explanation without intent to infringe.

Library of Congress Cataloging in Publication Data
Names: Sanzo, Karen, author.
Title: Strategies for developing and supporting school leaders : stepping stones to great leadership / Karen Sanzo.
Description: New York, NY : Routledge, 2016. | Includes bibliographical references.
Identifiers: LCCN 2015039783| ISBN 9781138914704 (hardback) | ISBN 9781138914711 (pbk.) | ISBN 9781315690643 (ebook)
Subjects: LCSH: School principals—Training of. | School administrators—Training of. | Educational leadership. | School management and organization.
Classification: LCC LB2831.9 .S26 2016 | DDC 371.2/012—dc23
LC record available at http://lccn.loc.gov/2015039783

ISBN: 978-1-138-91470-4 (hbk)
ISBN: 978-1-138-91471-1 (pbk)
ISBN: 978-1-315-69064-3 (ebk)

Typeset in Optima
by Keystroke, Station Road, Codsall, Wolverhampton

Contents

Preface vii

1 Developing Great Leaders 1
2 Creating a Leadership Development System 10
3 Leadership Development Pathways 23
4 Partnering for Success 36
5 Grow-Your-Own Model: Aspiring Leaders 50
6 Grow-Your-Own Model: Current Leaders 61
7 Mentoring and Coaching 72
8 Additional Features of a Leadership Development System ... 85
9 Adding to Your Leadership Development Toolkit 103

References 136

Preface

Why *Strategies for Developing and Supporting School Leaders?*

Great leaders matter in the lives of students. It is my hope through this book that you are able to learn more about practices you can use in your own organization to increase the capacity of school leaders. In this book you will discover strategies, processes, and holistic initiatives to help you better prepare current and aspiring leaders to meet the needs of a diverse student population. It is critical to provide current and aspiring school leaders with meaningful, engaging, and relevant professional learning opportunities to help promote highly effective schools and districts.

In my work with educational organizations across the United States I have frequently encountered the questions of "What do I do?" and "How do I do this?" in reference to preparing and developing school leaders. There is an amazing wealth of strategies, activities, and initiatives in use across the US and globally to prepare high quality school leaders that support exemplary learning organizations. What is lacking is a source that curates these approaches, as well as a cohesive framework to think about how to engage in this important work. This book represents the first phase in this process to bring together various tools into one resource, along with articulating a framework, to enable educational organizations to create an effective professional development system for school leaders. It is impossible to describe every strategy, process, and concept within one book. However, with knowledge and exposure to a broad array of support mechanisms, districts and other educational organizations are better situated to create an effective Leadership Development System.

Special Features of the Book

In this book I explore why great leaders matter and argue for an ecological understanding of leadership development. I have developed a Leadership Development Ecological Framework that can help educational organizations transition from an industrial age mode of thinking about leadership development to a contemporary construct of our inherently adaptive-thinking oriented educational systems (Wielkiewicz & Stelzner, 2005). I share literature around the powerful impacts leaders have on students and provide an overview of what we currently know about leadership development and support for school leaders. We have to know why we care about developing the best leaders possible in our schools and some of the background on how to do this. Within a Leadership Development Ecological Framework, I provide strategies, processes, protocols, and activities that can be implemented to support and develop school leaders. Some of these will be simple and others more complex and nuanced. Some may fit perfectly into your current organization's leadership development paradigm, while others may require adaptation (of either the strategy or the organizational approach, or both). These practices are drawn directly from the field and provided by PK-12 educators, higher education faculty, and other development organizations.

One of the biggest hurdles we face in school districts across the nation is a lack of time and resources to identify development and support activities that truly work and are grounded in research and proven best practices. These processes and activities are "out there" and some districts and organizations working to develop leaders are finding great success in a variety of initiatives to develop the best possible principals, assistant principals, and other school leaders. These range from the simple (such as monthly breakfasts) to the more complex (such as comprehensive pipeline initiatives that support leaders such as aspiring teacher leaders, emerging leaders who are assistant principals, and developing current principals at various stages of their career). Through this book I will identify these and discuss how to integrate the ones that work for your district into your own Leadership Development System.

Preface

How this Book is Organized

In Chapter 1 I explore why great leaders matter in our schools and why leadership development initiatives are a critical part of creating a high-performing school district. Within this chapter I begin to discuss who are considered to be leaders in a system and which individuals should be part of a cohesive Leadership Development System. I then provide some background on leadership preparation and development. Chapter 2 further illustrates concepts to consider when creating a Leadership Development System and introduces the Leadership Development Ecological Framework that can serve as an informative framework for Leadership Development System designers.

Chapter 3 examines different pathways educational organizations have articulated for their own Leadership Development Systems. It guides you through various pipeline and pathway concepts to help you articulate your own system, while providing examples in use by educators across the United States. Partnerships are a vital component of an effective Leadership Development System, and Chapter 4 expands upon how to partner for success. Tools for developing and sustaining partnerships around leadership development are provided.

Leadership Development Systems that are effective involve the entire continuum of school leaders, beginning with aspiring and emerging leaders. In Chapter 5, the concept of developing aspiring leader programs through a "grow-your-own" model is examined. Initial questions to explore while considering the aspiring leadership developmental needs in the organization are shared and the different types of aspiring leaders are discussed. Examples from the field around preparing aspiring school leaders are also provided. Chapter 6 looks at the "grow-your-own" concept through the lens of current educational leadership development needs. Different forms of professional development are shared, with several real-life examples that can be applied in your own Leadership Development System.

There are a number of program features that should be included in a Leadership Development System. These include the integration of mentors and coaches into the support structure. Chapter 7 helps you to understand the differences between the roles of mentors and coaches. Chapter 8 expands upon three additional program features that were raised earlier in the book: cohorts, field-based experiences, and problem-based learning. All of these program features are found in high-quality Leadership Development Systems. The final chapter provides additional tools, strategies, and resources that are being used by educational leaders in Leadership Development Systems throughout the United States.

Developing Great Leaders

Every school deserves a great leader. Highly effective principals are at the heart of successful schools and those leaders are part of dynamic leadership teams well equipped to meet the unique challenges of diverse school settings. Leithwood et al. (2004) have noted that no school improvement initiative they observed ever happened without strong principals. How these principals became great leaders and how these teams became successful working together can most likely be attributed to hard work, perseverance, and powerful professional learning experiences. These experiences were more than likely varied, differentiated, and based on practical application of skills grounded in research and theory.

> Strong leaders are not born—they are continually developed through iterative professional learning opportunities.

The challenge for many school districts is they are still searching for the elusive, and generally singular, "powerful professional learning experience" that will "fix" their own schools and districts. The reality is there is no one best fit for professional learning for current and aspiring school leaders that will make them successful. What must happen in order for school personnel to be developed into great leaders is the implementation of a combination of deliberate and well-crafted activities and processes informed by research, theory, a deep understanding of the unique needs of students in their community, and a sensitivity to adult learning principles that enable school districts to develop effective principals, assistant principals, and other school leaders. In Chapter 2 you will read more about the Leadership Development Ecological Framework that can be applied to a district's approach to leadership development.

Students Need Great Leaders

Students must have the best school leaders possible. Anything less is unacceptable. The challenge is that districts are overloaded with competing initiatives, requiring time and resources. This means that focusing solely on activities and processes for developing and supporting the evolving growth needs of current and aspiring school leaders often takes a back seat to other professional learning activities focused on instructional and content-based initiatives. "Sit-and-get" development that does not adhere to adult learning theory, is not engaging, and does not fit into a coherent leadership support structure is doomed to fail from the onset.

While the role of the school leader is critical to the success of schools, there is ongoing concern that not enough is being done to effectively prepare leaders for their jobs (Murphy, 2005; Young, Petersen, & Short, 2002). Instruction and content are critical and professional development must be provided on these, but there should not be an either/or approach to developing and supporting school leaders. Rather, professional learning can and should be embedded in our schools and other district development practices. Design matters in professional learning and should be taken into account.

Leadership development and support initiatives cannot play second fiddle to other priorities. What this means is that while there is a very real need to focus on instructional areas such as how to integrate effective formative assessment practices into the classroom, how teachers can effectively implement a new language arts curriculum, understanding a mathematics curriculum, and other instructional topics, without developing our leaders and helping them understand *how* to develop teachers and lead the instructionally focused initiatives will not be successful. If we do not provide support for our current leaders, develop our emerging leaders, and design a Leadership Development System, then we are doomed to fail our students by placing sub-par leaders in their schools. Effective leaders make a very real difference in the lives of children, helping to promote structures and facilitate processes in schools that allow students to be successful. This book serves as a resource for districts and other educational organizations seeking to enhance, develop, or reimagine their own school leader professional development mechanisms.

Great Leaders Make a Difference

Great leaders make a positive difference in schools. The role of the instructional leader is essential "in creating and fostering the conditions for success" (Sanzo, Myran, & Caggiano, 2015, p. 12). Effective school leadership significantly influences student academic achievement and the overall success of schools (Hattie, 2009; Leithwood et al., 2004; Robinson, Lloyd, & Rowe, 2008).

> Leadership is second only to classroom instruction among all school-related factors that contribute to what students learn at school . . . The total (direct and indirect) effects of leadership on student learning account for about a quarter of total school effects.
> (Leithwood et al., 2004, p. 5)

High-needs schools see an even greater impact by principals than low-poverty schools, with almost twice as large an effect on value-added scores (Davis & Wilson, 2000). The direct impact of leaders on student success is limited, but the indirect impact does "affect the social context in which teachers and students work" (Bellamy, Crockett, & Nordengren, 2014, p. 8). Therefore it is important to include all types of leaders within your Leadership Development System, focusing on distributing leadership responsibilities. "Because many members of school communities affect school conditions, it is not surprising that among administrators, teachers, students, and families, leadership in the most effective schools is widely shared" (Bellamy, Crockett, & Nordengren, 2014, p. 9).

School leaders impact student learning and school success in many different ways. Researchers looking into the impact of school leaders have revealed behaviors and skills that influence student achievement. Grissom and Loeb (2011) found five broad domains of principal action: (1) instructional management; (2) organizational management; (3) internal relations; (4) external relations; and (5) administrative duties. These five categories encompass responsibilities such as supporting classroom instruction and curricula, oversight of facilities and school resources, developing a positive relationship with the internal and external school community, and tasks such as scheduling and discipline. A meta-analysis by Robinson, Lloyd, and Rowe (2008) found specifically that instructionally focused responsibilities such as observations and professional development contribute to the effectiveness of principals.

Understanding Leadership Development Initiatives

Preparing aspiring leaders and developing emerging and current school leaders has been an area of focus for a number of years for professional development initiatives. Within the past 10–15 years there has been an even higher level of focus around this area. It is not surprising that there is so much focus now on school leaders, and in particular school principals. This is in response, in part, to heightened accountability systems. Within the United States, for example, increased accountability levers have targeted the role of the school principal, and many states have developed leadership evaluation systems that include student achievement as a measure through which the leader is evaluated. There has been a collective outcry for something more to be done to support schools through the development of high-quality school leaders.

The increased attention on the role of the school leader has caused both leadership preparation programs and post-credentialing programs to face an increased level of scrutiny. Attention is not bad and, in fact, has been a motivator to provide the best support available for school leaders, as well as to be highly innovative in constructing new and creative ways to provide additional training. Another positive outcome of this attention has been a better understanding of different practices being used as part of development initiatives. Burke, Marx, and Lowenstein (2012) argue these leadership development initiatives require "innovative collaboration that is contextually-situated, personally relevant, and informed by authentic issues and experiences of leadership practice" (p. 113). The types of strategies, activities, and processes used must be contextually based—in essence adaptive—and integrated into the larger (open) system.

Who Participates in Leadership Development Initiatives?

Who is developed has also seen a change in focus, in addition to changes in how leadership development and support are provided. There are different types of leadership positions in an educational organization and while it appears the primary development attention still rests on the identification and cultivation of traditional building level leadership positions (principal and assistant principal), other leadership positions are also receiving increased attention. These include teacher leader, instructional coach, curriculum director, and principal supervisor.

Teacher leader roles have expanded almost exponentially over the past decade. This could be in response to a better understanding of the power and impact of shared and distributed leadership models and how critical teacher leaders are in helping schools function effectively. Sharing leadership with teachers is a strong motivator for staff (Davis & Wilson, 2000). With this understanding comes the realization that the role of principal and assistant principal are almost untenable positions without additional site-based support. Whatever the case, it is clear that teacher leadership positions play a critical role in the overall operation of a school. These individuals must be included in a cohesive Leadership Development System.

Coaching roles in the school setting and at the central office levels have also rapidly increased. Within the United States, there are a number of coaching models being used to help support teachers and leaders. The role of coach, often the instructional coach, is a quasi-administrative role and one that requires ongoing training and support, especially related to psychological principles around coaching and adult learning theory. We also see organizations external to school districts such as the New York City Leadership Academy, the National Institute for School Leadership, and Thinking Collaborative providing intense coaching support for schools and districts.

Central office leadership positions also fall on the leadership development continuum. In the past, central office leaders were not provided with as much development and support as building level leaders. This could be, in part, because of the traditional pathway of how a person became a leader at the central office. Once, the traditional pathway to the central office was through holding a principal position. Today that is no longer the case. While generally most principal supervisors have held a principal role, other central office positions such as curriculum director often do not require that same type of leadership experience. There are other roles, too, that do not require experience as a building level leader, including professional development coordinator and instructional coach. Therefore, professional development should be differentiated, individualized, and based on the background and experiences of each participant.

Consider this example from the field. A high school principal from a small rural school district describes different types of teacher leader roles and how he develops leadership capacity within his school using his limited fiscal and personnel resources.

Example from the Field

Progressive Leadership Development

Some of the formal practices that we employ at Windsor High School are the administrative aide position and our professional learning steering committee (PLSC). The administrative aide position is used for a teacher that shows leadership potential and gives them an opportunity to get a taste of administrative experience. Teachers in this position serve as quasi-assistant principals. They handle less severe discipline, testing software, grade book monitoring, and logistical tasks. Teachers on the PLSC represent different departments in our school and make a three-year commitment to lead cross-curricular groups in professional conversations and sharing of practices. The paradigm change that teachers have in these programs is priceless. Teachers are exposed to how difficult it is to lead leaders. Teachers are accustomed to leading their classrooms in solitude. So PLSC members have to take a new view and approach when leading teachers. Administrative aides see the challenges and successes other teachers experience when different protocols are, or are not, followed and how different teaching styles and personalities can work. Administrative aides are exposed to the multiple influences that pull leaders in different directions. The challenge of "gray area" decisions present growth opportunities for these teachers.

> The non-formal practices I have with the titled and untitled leaders in my school stem from building strong relationships of trust. In a small school, we have a minimal staff, so teacher leaders are essential to keep the school moving forward. Spending time developing teachers with conferences, delegated tasks, supporting their professional growth, and constant two-way feedback has helped. There is some professional pushing involved in all of this. My teacher leaders and I want to get better and want our school to get better; so, frank feedback is appreciated and expected. This is where the trust comes in. When unfiltered feedback is a norm, feelings will get hurt if we don't trust that we are all pushing for improvement.
> Danny Soderholm, Principal, Windsor High School, Isle of Wight County Public Schools, Virginia

A Brief Background on Leadership Preparation and Development

The pathway to school leadership was generally a predictable one several decades ago and had not changed in terms of the path for quite some time. Teachers attended a formal credentialing program that provided them with the requisite knowledge base and skill set to transition into an assistant principal role, or sometimes directly into a principal role. Typically the credentialing program was a formal university master's degree program. Upon completion of the program and securing a leadership position, training then became the domain of the district in which the leader worked. There was a distinct bifurcation between pre-licensure and post-licensure development. Pre-licensure training was the domain of universities and, upon graduation, the credentialed educators transitioned into the domain of the school district. There was little partnering, connection, or collaboration. This is not to say it did not happen, but generally these two entities were separated.

Educational administration preparation programs were not immune from popular criticism and the educational reform efforts of the latter half of the 20th century. A decade before the famous 1983 "A Nation at Risk" report in the United States, the *Series on Administrator Preparation* in 1972 expressed concerns about leadership preparation programs, including structural critiques, recruitment challenges, and internship concerns (Lutz & Ferrante, 1972). About fifteen years later, the University Council for Educational Administration (UCEA) released a report that again highlighted what seemed to be pervasive criticisms about university-based leadership preparation programs that included internship experiences, content, and lack of sequencing (Hale & Moorman, 2003). More recent critics continue to highlight issues around university preparation programs, citing many of the same issues as in previous reports (Levine, 2005; Murphy & Vriesenga, 2006; US Department of Education, 2004).

One could imagine with such voluminous criticism and concern about leadership preparation programs that university-based leadership preparation programs might have become obsolete. This has not been the case. Rather than continuing to repeat the status quo (and perhaps phase themselves out of the leadership development equation because of failure to adapt to changes in education), a revolution of sorts has been seen on the preparation side of leadership development. Leadership preparation programs across the United States, for example, have experienced substantive transformations in response to national concerns about how school leaders are prepared. A number of national organizations and state entities are helping to catalyze the change effort and create high-quality programs that meet the needs of school districts, schools themselves, and other educational agencies such as charter school organizations. Additionally, states such as Kentucky and Alabama have mandated comprehensive redesigns of university-based leadership preparation programs, with some requiring formal partnerships between universities and districts. National leadership standards have been revised (Interstate School Leaders Licensure Consortium) to help better inform practice at the pre-credentialing stage.

In addition, there are newer organizations that have also been formed to provide leadership development training for aspiring school leaders. There has been a proliferation of non-university-based programs influencing the preparation (and at times providing the preparation and credentialing) for aspiring and current school leaders.

On the post-credential side, national-level organizations have been a primary driver for the types of professional development opportunities available to schools, districts, and other organizations for quite some time. These organizations continue to be powerful influences on the types of content provided through professional development (such as the National Association of Secondary School Principals, National Association of

Elementary School Principals, and ASCD) as well as how the professional development is implemented (Learning Forward). They continue to offer powerful training opportunities for school leaders. Educators responsible for designing and implementing a Leadership Development System should continually monitor these organizations for national trends and areas of focus, and utilize their collective work as a part of the system. Many offer opportunities to partner with the organizations, too. Additionally, many of the same aforementioned non-university-based organizations have forayed into the leadership development side (post-aspiring leader) to integrate their own work into development initiatives. These, too, can become a part of a system's professional learning initiatives.

Great leaders matter and developing outstanding school leaders is critical to the success of schools. While it would be ideal to have one singular approach to preparing effective leaders, there is no one "right way" to address an organization's leadership development and preparation needs. This is due to many reasons, including the evolving roles of leaders and different types of leadership jobs within educational organizations. Districts and other organizations seeking to prepare high-quality school leaders will benefit immensely from leadership development initiatives that have an articulated focus in terms of the scope of job roles the system will cover.

2 | Creating a Leadership Development System

Creating a Leadership Development System is challenging, but incredibly rewarding when done correctly. "It is possible to build more cohesive leadership systems and . . . such efforts appear to be a promising approach to developing school leaders engaged in improving instruction" (Augustine et al., 2009, p. xvii). The results of the effective system not only impact the adults that participate in the development initiatives, but also have lasting impacts on the staff they work with and, ultimately, the students in schools. Remember, the impact of leaders is tremendous—and therefore creating and implementing an effective professional Leadership Development System that includes all leaders and aspiring leaders is critical and should not be approached lightly.

When crafting your system, keep in mind the findings from a 2009 study commissioned by the Wallace Foundation around cohesive leadership systems. The eight strategies found to be the most critical for building a cohesive Leadership Development System were (Augustine et al., 2009, pp. xviii–xix):

1. Building trust
2. Creating formal and informal networks
3. Fostering communications
4. Exerting pressure and influence
5. Promoting improved quality of leadership policies and initiatives
6. Building capacity for the work
7. Identifying strong individuals with political and social capital to lead the work
8. Connecting to other reform efforts.

It may be the case that instead of creating a new system, your educational organization is modifying an existing system. Whatever the situation may be, it is important the initiative be systemic and coordinated. Organizations need to design an approach that is meaningful and makes a lasting impact on participants and the organization itself (this includes students, staff, and stakeholders). The Leadership Development System must be a part of one cohesive system and not separate efforts by multiple entities. Too often development initiatives in districts happen haphazardly with multiple departments offering training on multiple topics, often not talking to each other or coordinating efforts. A district leader may question why an initiative failed and blame it on the initiative itself, rather than on the way the professional development on the topic was delivered and how many different departments were involved with competing delivery mechanisms.

Consider the implementation of communities of practice—known often as Professional Learning Communities (PLCs)—within districts and schools. How often have you heard a story about this not being successful or an inconsistent implementation across schools and grade levels? Communities of practice are grounded in research and speak to the adaptive nature of schools. Organizations that implement these communities with fidelity see great success. However, it is the unfortunate case that many PLC efforts have not been successful. This is not because PLCs do not work. They do. Rather, the majority of the time when PLCs do not work, it is because of the implementation of the PLC initiative. Perhaps one or two departments are responsible for sharing how to "run" PLCs with principals, who in turn share this with assistant principals and the leadership teams in schools, who then provide inconsistent training because of their lack of training. The problem is compounded when curriculum departments provide training on their own programs and initiatives, often without delivering this through the PLC model (norms, protocols, etc.). With conflicting training initiatives for school leaders comes a diluted understanding of how to effectively facilitate quality PLC meetings, and often these meetings devolve into meetings that are not instructionally focused, lack rigor and lack utilization of protocols, and are more managerial and top down in practice.

The development structure must take into account the unique personnel needs and the evolving needs of the district (again, including students, staff, and stakeholders). What has tended to happen in many organizations is that development initiatives are not subsumed under one overarching umbrella that deftly articulates and defines the types of practices needing to take place for leadership development. Often you find competing initiatives that vie for the time of leaders and do not take full advantage of internal capacity and resources (as well as external capacity and resource options). Additionally, these competing initiatives may operationalize their approaches to development in many different ways and are counterproductive.

> ### *Example from the Field*
>
> ### *Different Approaches to Developing Leaders*
>
> My favorite way to develop leaders is to find specific methods where they can model instructional leadership for their faculties and peer administrators. To be specific, administrative meetings, principals meetings, and even division wide convocations should be models of instruction where current leaders set an example for all of their colleagues through modeling.
>
> The purpose of each principals meeting is to develop skills that serve principals when they return to their buildings. For example, last spring we wanted to make sure that our principals moved beyond data mining and testing to explore non-measurable qualities. We utilized two principals to teach a lesson for our administrative team. The lesson focused on empathy. By using dyslexia as an example, the goal was to create an understanding of what it was like to have this disability. Many times we sympathize with the needs of our scholars, but only when we can empathize with them do we authentically connect. Our principals used the analogy of being in a boat and someone falls overboard. One who sympathizes acknowledges the water must be cold and deep, while the person who empathizes jumps in the water and tries to experience the cold and deep water with them. Our principals engaged in instructional activities to support this premise.
>
> In addition to principals meetings, we involve current and emerging leaders in convocation. Convocation is the single opportunity

annually to get all of our employees in the division together. Specifically, our current leaders and emerging leaders involve all employees as they teach all employees the six objectives in our division wide strategic plan. The leaders model instruction through the use of technology by means of Tweet Chats, small groups (think, pair, share), and even getting all employees moving during the lesson. Convocation allows us an opportunity for our leaders to model instruction and hone their leadership skills while providing direction to the entire school division.

Dr. Mark Lineburg, Superintendent of Winchester Public Schools in Virginia, shares above some of the different ways he involves all leaders in the development system and strategies for peers to support one another.

Technical and Adaptive Structures

These challenges are both technical and adaptive in nature and require Leadership Development System structures that are both technical and adaptive. Technical challenges and structures are those that "can be implemented by current know-how" and addressed "through the application of authoritative expertise and through the organization's current structures, procedures, and ways of doing things" (Heifetz, Grashow, & Linsky, 2009, p. 19). Adaptive challenges and structures, on the other hand, are tackled and built "through changes in people's priorities, beliefs, habits, and loyalties. Making progress requires going beyond any authoritative expertise to mobilize discovery, shedding certain entrenched ways, tolerating losses, and generating the new capacity to thrive anew" (Heifetz, Grashow, & Linsky, 2009, p. 19). Obviously leadership development challenges are not neatly split between technical and adaptive and often are interconnected (Heifetz, Grashow, & Linsky, 2009).

In essence an organization's approach to articulating a meaningful development system is complex and must be responsive to both the individual and the organization. Therefore, those designing preparation and development initiatives must give careful consideration to structures of the system and the needs—both technical and adaptive—of the system being addressed. "Today, high-performing organizations must constantly problem-solve in an ad hoc, rather than a straightforward and predictable fashion" (Stephens & Boland, 2015, p. 220).

An Ecological Approach to Leadership Development

This book is designed as an informative guide to aid districts and others involved in preparing and developing great school leaders. In this book are a number of valuable resources that can aid in the construction—or redesign—of a Leadership Development System in an organization. It is important to use these tools and strategies within a strategic framework.

A Leadership Development Ecological Framework is one such framework that can be immeasurably helpful. Without a framework, any effort to improve a system will more than likely not be as successful as it could be, or could potentially fail (fail in its implementation, fail to be sustainable, etc.). The framework provides a structure for your plan, a way of thinking about the organization of the plan, and helps you with the path forward. Schools, districts, and other educational organizations are not isolated from the broader community and as such must be cognizant of the varying connections across organizations. The Leadership Development Ecological Framework takes this interconnectedness into account and helps the organization keep that present in planning efforts. The interdependence of educational agencies spans beyond schools, individual districts, and individual educational organizations, and often mirrors the national and global connectivity of society. Therefore, it is critical professional learning designers targeting ways to best impact the developmental needs of current, emerging, and aspiring school leaders engage in their work through an "ecological" framework. But what does an "ecological" framework mean?

Leadership Development Ecological Framework

It used to be the case that schools and districts operated more like factory assembly lines. (And some may argue this is still the case. However, the adaptive needs of society demand something radically different from the antiquated factory model of schools). In these assembly-line type schools teachers functioned like line workers and students worked through the assembly line like products being assembled and moved toward a "complete" status. Teachers functioned almost as if they were in compartments (or silos), working independently from each other, with administrators serving as supervisors of the line. Think of the way many schools are still physically structured;—if you lift the roof off you will see individual, disconnected rooms, students moving from one grade to the next—like an assembly line in a factory.

However, what is different today than in the past, even with a physical "egg-crate" model of schools still present structurally, is the function of schools and how many, if not most, operate. Schools and systems are complex. There is a great deal of interaction between and across teachers and leaders. Students are being charged as active agents of their own learning through formative assessment practices, goal setting, and communication with teachers in a way unheard of years ago (Sanzo, Myran, & Caggiano, 2015). Passivity on the part of the learner and an almost dictatorial and one-way teaching approach from times past have been proven to be an ineffective way of promoting engagement and deep learning. There is a fluidity to the school, an organic feel, and palpable change to the way schools operate. Today, educators are connected with one another and organizations are connected to varying degrees. It is this connectivity that promotes (and requires) an ecological approach to the way educational organizations function, including the Leadership Development System.

Educators and organizations must work within the constraints and resources of the system, which is an open one that can incorporate the resources of other organizations in a collaborative manner. Again, connectivity is critical. Systems must adopt an adaptive orientation to leadership development and assume a learning mindset to the work, as well as utilize ongoing feedback of lessons learned directly into the Leadership Development System. "The ecological approach inherently recognizes the complexity of our world, while simultaneously helping us understand it" (Allen, Stelzner, & Wielkiewicz, 1998, p. 68).

A Quick Background on Ecological Frameworks in Leadership

Think about ecology. Ecology is about living things and how those living things interact with one another and with their environments. Schools and districts are living systems—they are more than desks, books, buses, computers, and tables. Educational institutions are created and sustained for and by people. Unfortunately, educational institutions have been treated in a mechanistic way (think factory model), with assumptions (often unspoken) that people should behave like machines and operate in a line-order fashion with predictable responses like machines. This ignores the ecology of the system—the living system, the emotional side of people, the psychology behind students and adults, the social components of education, and that people are interconnected.

Just like ecosystems studied in science class, educational organizations are their own ecosystems. Separate ecosystems can be impacted by internal and external change. Sometimes these changes are slow, but "other times, change is abrupt, disorganizing, or turbulent" (Folke et al., 2005, p. 442). Because of ongoing changes in education, educators (and Leadership Development Systems) need to be adaptable, as the "capacity of ecosystems to remain within desired states in the face of abrupt change seems to have been reduced as a consequence of human actions" (p. 442). Adaptable ecosystems are resilient and resilient educational systems will be robust enough to adapt to changes and be sustainable. Otherwise, poorly adapted systems falter (consider schools that cannot keep up with changing standards and are failing and potentially subject to state takeover or closure).

An approach to leadership development through the lens of an ecological framework requires professional learning designers to consider the role of people themselves within (and outside) the institution and how they are connected. In addition, resources within an ecosystem are often finite, unless other resources are brought in and either shared or co-used by another person (or school, organization, . . .). In this way, schools must understand how to capitalize on internal resources and recycle those resources, while at the same time understanding what resources outside of the system are viable options to use. Because ecosystems, and educational organizations, are open systems, they do engage with other systems (Allen, Stelzner, & Wielkiewicz, 1998). Schools connect with other schools, districts interact with other districts, and so on. The open nature of a healthy ecosystem allows for "feedback loops that lead to self-organizing properties that will allow the organization to adapt to the larger systems of which it is a part" (Allen, Stelzner, & Wielkiewicz, 1998, p. 70). Consider the feedback loop in the ecosystem as a larger form of formative assessment that is now

Creating a Leadership Development System

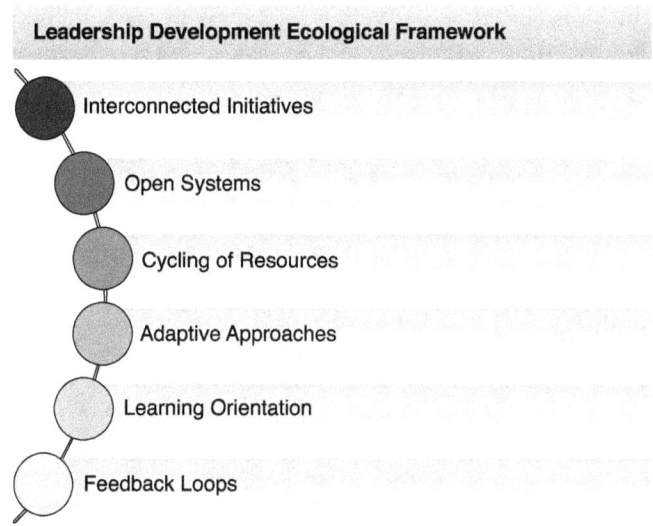

Figure 2.1 Leadership Development Ecological Framework
Source: Author

popular and prevalent in schools. The same concept applies. The use of feedback loops to improve the organization requires a learning orientation to truly use the feedback and make changes. The framework suggested in this book is detailed in Figure 2.1.

Interconnected Initiatives—Consider the pebble thrown into the water. The one pebble makes a number of ripples in the water. If you throw five pebbles into the same body of water, each pebble makes a number of ripples that impact the other ripples from all of the other pebbles. Expanding this metaphor, what happens in one professional development initiative impacts what happens in another, whether it was the intent of the two to interact or not. If five principals in your system are involved in multiple coaching projects, multiple professional development projects, and with multiple organizations in their work and training, they will all impact each other. A well-crafted professional development system will ensure there are dove-tailed initiatives that embrace the interconnected possibilities.

Open Systems—Schools and districts are not insulated or isolated organizations. There are a number of organizations in the field that can interact with one another and impact each other. Understanding these organizations and how institutions interact with one another is important and can bring great value to the Leadership Development System.

Cycling of Resources—Internal capacity should be capitalized upon in an organization. This is most important when considering the organization's most valuable resource—the people. Leadership Development Systems need to promote and support leadership growth internally, while at the same time engaging with external resource opportunities like other schools and districts, universities, leadership organizations, and further possibilities.

Adaptive Approaches—The organization must be adaptive and able to respond to the various and unique needs of the stakeholders in the system. An adaptive orientation allows the system to be flexible and modify (or completely change) an approach or initiative. An adaptive system understands that there are often different solutions to a challenge and multiple ways to enact professional learning. Systems must move beyond the status quo.

Learning Orientation—Professional development is "learning-focused." Collaboration and collaborative inquiry allow educators to alter their practice (Fullan, 2005). Adopting a learning mindset in professional development initiatives not only impacts the participants themselves, but also allows the improvement of the Leadership Development System as a whole. Adopting a learning orientation to professional development helps to ensure the success and sustainability of the work.

Feedback Loops—Iterative formative feedback increases a system's ability to continuously improve by understanding the impact of the professional learning initiatives and making modifications (or changing). Effective professional development systems continually monitor and assess the efficacy of learning initiatives and make improvements to the efforts. Feedback "capitalizes on success and mitigates weaknesses by only promoting what was effective to subsequent iterations of the process" (Sanzo, Myran, & Caggiano, 2015, p. 86).

Changing a System

You may be making modifications to an existing Leadership Development System, or completely reimagining one. Regardless of the magnitude of change, more than likely there will be some challenges. Change is difficult for many people and anticipating some of the challenges to the change effort, including resistance and structural issues, will help with a smooth transition to the new development system. In addition, it will aid in sustaining the new system.

Conducting the Leadership Development Needs Assessment is an important initial step in engaging in a re-visioning process for the new Leadership Development System. This tool is located in Chapter 9 and provides a baseline picture of leadership development within an organization. The assessment tool offers a starting point from which to evaluate needs. Leadership Development System designers are able to better understand the previous and current systems, and to avoid losing valuable pieces from the past initiatives that worked well. This is part of the cycling of resources through the Leadership Development Ecological Framework. An ecological mindset and approach will assuredly aid the Leadership Development System designers with the process.

"Disequilibrium" is inherent in an adaptive change process (Heifetz, Grashow, & Linsky, 2009). "Honoring the reality that adaptive processes will be accompanied by distress means having compassion for the pain that comes with deep change" (Heifetz, Grashow, & Linsky, 2009, p. 29). This type of "second-order" change to a Leadership Development System—a holistic approach—is probably different from what many are accustomed to in an organization, as well as some of the more innovative and different approaches to leadership development advocated for in this book. "Second-order change goes against the status quo, is uncomfortable, and requires a deep investment in time and effort in order for the initiative to take root" (Sanzo, Myran, & Caggiano, 2015, p. 63).

Sustaining the Leadership Development System Change

Sustainable change effort "requires both perseverance and flexibility to develop organizational resiliency toward further change adoption" (Browne-Ferrigno, 2014, p. 25).

Authentic and intentional implementation of the new Leadership Development System using a Leadership Development Ecological Framework is instrumental in sustaining the change. In 2005, Fullan

Creating a Leadership Development System

identified eight essential elements to sustain innovative change initiatives. Because of the prevalence of Fullan's work throughout PK-12 education, his framework is used and cross-walked with the Leadership Development Ecological Framework below to help Leadership Development System designers better reflect on crafting and implementing a sustainable system.

Table 2.1 Sustainable Innovation Chart—Fullan and the LDEF

Fullan's Eight Elements	Description of Elements for Sustainable Innovative Change	Leadership Development Ecological Framework Constructs
Public Service with a Moral Purpose	Collective efforts, focus on social justice for individuals, organizations, and environments	• Interconnected Initiatives • Open Systems • Feedback Loops
Commitment to Changing Context at All Levels	Changing context to create a sustainable effort requires participation and interactions from every person in the system at every level in the system. There must be a shared commitment.	• Interconnected Initiatives • Open Systems • Adaptive Approaches • Learning Orientation
Lateral Capacity Building through Networks	Systemic change requires vertical and horizontal networking and capacity building within and across stakeholder groups.	• Interconnected Initiatives • Open Systems • Cycling of Resources • Adaptive Approaches • Learning Orientation • Feedback Loops
Intelligent Accountability and Vertical Relationships	Problems inevitably arise in any change initiative and impact groups across the system. Joint problem solving, open communication, and transparency across vertical relationships are necessary.	• Interconnected Initiatives • Adaptive Approaches • Learning Orientation • Feedback Loops

Creating a Leadership Development System

Fullan's Eight Elements	Description of Elements for Sustainable Innovative Change	Leadership Development Ecological Framework Constructs
Deep Learning	Adaptive systems that are responsive to change efforts promote deep and sustained learning around the innovative initiatives. These efforts can produce failed attempts, but deep learning organizations embrace cycles of continuous improvement and learn and improve upon the system through an adaptive approach and mindset.	• Interconnected Initiatives • Cycling of Resources • Adaptive Approaches • Learning Orientation • Feedback Loops
Dual Commitments to Short-Term and Long-Term Results	Sustainability of change efforts requires commitment to incremental goal setting and long-term visioning.	• Interconnected Initiatives • Learning Orientation • Feedback Loops
Cyclical Energizing	There is a pattern of change that involves energy expended on short-term efforts, followed by longer periods of stability that allow deep reflection to promote sustainability.	• Interconnected Initiatives • Cycling of Resources • Open Systems • Feedback Loops
The Long Lever of Leadership	All leaders across the system must be involved as change agents in the effort. Sustainability is the responsibility of everyone in the organization.	• Interconnected Initiatives • Open Systems • Learning Orientation

Source: Table adapted from Browne-Ferrigno (2014) and informed by Fullan (2005)

Creating a Leadership Development System

A cohesive Leadership Development System adopts an adaptive orientation and approach to addressing the preparation needs for current, emerging, and aspiring school leaders. Through the use of an Ecological Framework to leadership development, educational organizations can address the complexity of skills and knowledge needed for today's school leaders and craft a system that effectively cultivates exemplary educational leaders. The framework employs an ecosystem-like mindset that includes the acknowledgment of and understanding of: interconnected initiatives, open systems, cycling of resources, adaptive approaches, learning orientations, and feedback loops. Leadership Development System designers should be cautious about potential challenges involving change initiatives, but not hesitant to implement change. Sustainable change is possible through a well-crafted and implemented Leadership Development System.

Leadership Development Pathways

There are different ways to think about, conceptualize, and talk about a Leadership Development System. Within your own system you will want to succinctly articulate the type of system you are using. You can develop your own concept or use one of four that are prevalent (or becoming prevalent) in practice and literature. These are (Supovitz, 2014):

- succession planning
- leadership pipeline initiatives
- leadership pathways
- lattice for school leadership.

The system needs to reflect your organization's philosophical approach to leadership development. In order to do this, you must know:

- Who are the leaders in your organization?
- Who is responsible for developing leaders in your system?
- What is the role of professional development in your organization to prepare and develop leaders?
- Do you want to prepare aspiring leaders or wait until they already have their leadership credentials from an outside organization?
- What is your vision and mission for the organization and how do these connect to your philosophy of leadership development?
- What are your organization's values and beliefs?

- What are the dispositions you are seeking in new leaders and veteran leaders?
- What is your belief in student learning?

In addition to these questions, you should develop organization specific questions to explore as you craft your own system.

Below is an example of one district's philosophical approach to developing their school leaders.

> ## *Example from the Field*
>
> ## *Leadership Development Philosophy*
>
> Gwinnett County Public Schools has been nationally recognized for their work around leadership development. The district won the Broad Prize for Urban Education in 2010 and 2014 and was recognized for their Quality-Plus Leader Academy. Gwinnett is also one of the Wallace Foundation's "Principal Pipeline" districts. The Bush Institute at the George W. Bush Presidential Center featured Gwinnett County Public Schools in a case study in 2015 because of their work around leadership development.
>
> Guiding the Leadership Development System is an articulated philosophy of school leadership. "Principals in GCPS are expected to serve first and foremost as instructional leaders and focus intensely on the academic performance of their students" (Bush Institute, 2015, p. 12).
>
> The district has adopted the following as part of their philosophy around leadership development (Bush Institute, 2015):
>
> 1. School leadership is a strategic priority;
> 2. Create conditions enabling school leaders to be successful through driving school and student success; and
> 3. Create a robust leadership development pipeline.

Regardless of your organization's approach, the Leadership Development Ecological Framework needs to be borne in mind. Without doing so, the system will ignore critical factors that will impact the success and sustainability of the initiative. At some point in time the titles of these initiatives (succession planning, pipeline, pathways, lattice)—not the initiatives themselves—become semantics and branding of a concept. (Branding of your Leadership Development System is important and will be discussed later.) However, there are some features of each that are important to understand and consider when designing your own system. In this chapter you will learn about different systemic approaches to leadership development in order to better develop or adapt your system.

Who Is a Leader in Your System?

The first thing to understand in your system is: who are the people being developed? A well-crafted Leadership Development System takes into account human capital resources within the system and has a way of supporting each person on his or her professional continuum. It is the argument of this book that everyone in a system receives some sort of training related to leadership principles. Too often people are tasked with responsibilities requiring leadership training, but they are not provided with any support.

Consider the professional learning community example given in Chapter 1. Within the past ten years a shift in thinking has occurred about how adults interact with one another across grade level and content teams. It used to be the case that teachers were "left alone" to plan and rarely met as teams. When they did, it was to discuss more managerial functions—student discipline, field trips, and schedule changes for testing. This concept of teaming is now outdated and has been replaced by the introduction of the communities of practice literature (Lave and Wegner) and professional learning communities (popularized by Dufour and Eaker in 1998 with *Professional Learning Communities at Work: Best Practices for Enhancing Student Achievement*).

However, there have been challenges in implementing learning communities with fidelity. While there are many well-functioning teams within a learning community framework, there are others that do not function well at all. Often the case is that teachers were not given adequate training around working with adults in a team setting, the effective use of protocols, norm setting, and other factors contributing to effective communities of practice. Better training design could help mitigate problems that have surfaced in the implementation of these communities. Additionally, a better understanding of how this training was situated within a broader Leadership Development System would have assisted with implementation.

Consider a different example using department chairs and grade level chairs. Many times teachers are promoted to a "quasi-leadership" role in a chair position (department, grade level, content, etc.). They are promoted to this role for reasons such as they have exhibited leadership potential, are exemplary teachers and can model instructional practices for others, and have demonstrated collaborative teaming skills. Yet, many of these teacher leaders have not gone through degree programs for school leadership and have never been provided with training (for example around effective leadership, working collaboratively, and leading teams). Because of this, these teacher leaders often struggle in leading their assigned teams and become frustrated (as well as the team and principal being frustrated).

> If the point of teacher leadership is to improve teaching and learning, thrusting high-performing teachers into teacher leader roles without training does a double disservice. It takes teaching time away from the educators best prepared to accelerate student learning, and then handicaps their potential to lead colleagues to similar successes by failing to equip them with the skills they need.
> (Valdez, Broin, & Carroll, 2015, p. 6)

In both of these examples teachers are serving in leadership roles, but require training in order to meet expectations and school needs. Without support and being part of an intentional, sustained, and well-designed Leadership Development System, these teacher leaders will not be successful. These examples are shared because they, too, along with assistant principals, principals, and other leaders, need to be considered as part of the leadership team in the system.

How Are Leaders Developed?

We cannot assume every person will follow the same exact process for leadership development. For example, while some teacher leaders, such as those in the examples for PLC and chair roles, may be interested in becoming an assistant principal and one day a principal, you cannot assume everyone in a teacher leader role is automatically interested in transitioning to an assistant principal and/or principal role. Some building principals may want to eventually move into principal supervisor roles, while others may choose to remain at the building level and others again want to become instructional coaches or curriculum leaders (or, using an adaptive approach to leadership role constructs—a yet to be created leadership role that will one day be in existence). Succession planning and the creation of a Leadership Development System has to take into account that there are multiple leadership pathways, and a straight transition from teacher to assistant principal to principal is not the standard any more. The "new normal" in leadership development looks very different from the past. Supovitz (2014) has argued in his analysis of the England Leadership Development System "to move beyond a linear sequence of tidy steps to support leaders toward a more complex set of interdependent, mutually reinforcing activities initiated and supported at multiple levels across the educational system" (p. 29). Therefore, developing a variety of pathways and possibilities—a lattice according to Supovitz (2014)—is critical.

At the start of this chapter multiple ways to conceptualize a Leadership Development System were listed: succession planning, leadership pipeline initiatives, leadership pathways, and lattice. Throwing around these terms without defining them in your organization can be problematic, since lack of agreement on terms can cause a misunderstanding of purposes and approaches to the system. Of course there may be other descriptions and approaches to leadership development in the literature, too, but generally they will begin to overlap in concept, ideas, and methods. In some fashion or another, essentially, these are different pathways to leadership and ways of developing leaders. As mentioned earlier, to a degree it becomes semantics and branding—placing an organization's own stamp on the approach. Branding is important and should not be discounted when designing a system of leadership development.

How you brand your Leadership Development System not only helps to solidify it as a part of the consciousness of staff within the system, but also becomes a marketing and recruitment tool for outstanding educators who may be interested in joining the organization. You are not only developing a system for those you have working currently in the organization; you are developing a system for what the organization aspires to be and for those you hope to recruit. The Leadership Development System should always be adaptive, open to ideas, and use a learning orientation to feed back into the system. What you stand for and who you are is often exemplified in the brand and marketing approach to the Leadership Development System.

Example from the Field
Individual Leader Development

Dawn Carroll is a success story of growing a leader at WHS. When I arrived as principal at Windsor High School, the staff was (and, for that matter, still is) very seasoned. Teachers were happy in their current roles. They were experts in what they chose to do and operated in silos. Mrs. Carroll seemed unique for a number of reasons. She was a reading intervention specialist and a great cheer coach. These two positions highlighted three key attributes: 1, she was used to differentiating instruction for the specific needs of students for intervention purposes; 2, she worked well with other teachers; and 3, she had the organizational skills to run a complex organization that involved teacher, student, parent, and community support. Another unique aspect of Mrs. Carroll is that she handled all aspects of the cheer team herself. There was no "drama" that came from her team or team parents. I saw a lot of potential in Mrs. Carroll to be a leader in our school, but she did not see her potential. She often expressed doubt about her teaching, knowledge, and ability to lead other professionals.

During a reduction in force process we had the opportunity to re-arrange our staffing. This was the opportunity to move Mrs. Carroll into a teaching position. A long-tenured staff member was moved to another school to make room for Mrs. Carroll to have a full teaching load in our English department. I reminded her that she was chosen for the position because of her instructional skills and we just couldn't lose her. Under the weight of expectations to be a great teacher, she developed detailed and student-centered lesson plans. We told her how good she was and she believed it.

The following school year we asked her to step into the role of administrative aide. We had multiple coaching sessions about her career and taking the next step. It took about a year of coaching to convince her to enroll in an administrative licensure program. Currently, she is still coaching the cheerleading team, teaching a full load of English classes, serving as administrative aide, and taking classes to gain licensure as an administrator. The same attention to detail and organizational skills that she applies in her lessons and coaching, she applies to her administrative duties. She is constantly pushing those around her to do better and remain inquisitive to find a better method. As I've told her and others many times, "Some day soon, she will have my job."

> Danny Soderholm, Principal at Windsor High School in Isle of Wight County Public Schools, Virginia, shares his experience developing a staff member, Dawn Carroll, with incredible leadership potential at his high school. Above he describes an adaptive approach to his leadership development that employs a learning orientation to the process.

Understanding Approaches

This section will provide general definitions for each of the aforementioned leadership development approaches. If you have your own concept within your organization, you are encouraged to operationalize your definition for your approach, cross-map it with the following definitions, and overlay it with the Leadership Development Ecological Framework. From there you can better refine (or reimagine) your system.

Succession Planning—Succession planning is perhaps the oldest of the four approaches defined in this section in terms of thinking about leadership development. Organizations engage in succession planning initiatives to prepare for their future leadership needs—preparing a "deep bench" so people can be "called up" to leadership positions as people transition to new roles and others retire. "During succession a successor who possesses knowledge about social influencing processes and skill in applying that knowledge can have a substantial impact on the outcomes of his or her own succession practices and experience" (Issa Lahera & Normore, 2014, p. 7). Many educational organizations engage in formal succession planning for the role of the principalship, seeing the assistant principal position as a training (and proving ground) for the principalship. (Some argue the assistant principal role as currently conceived in many organizations has very little to do with the job of a principal and actually is not adequate training for a principal position.) Some consider teacher leaders and central office positions within the succession planning model, but often that is limited.

Leadership Pipeline—More recently, focus has centered around leadership pipelines. Again, most of the focus in the pipeline initiative is on cultivating strong building level leadership around the role of the principal. The Wallace Foundation, for example, has dedicated resources to a "Principal Pipeline Initiative" that explores different pipeline programs around leadership development. Moving from a succession planning mindset, where the focus is primarily on leaders already in the system, pipeline initiatives such as those the Wallace Foundation has sponsored are holistic in concept—"defined as including not only preservice preparation for aspiring principals, but also the hiring process and the evaluation and support that novice principals receive, as well as standards and expectations for principals" (Turnbull et al., 2013, p. 2). Pipeline initiatives are unique to the organization and take into account several of the concepts in an ecological approach to leadership development: interconnected initiatives, open systems (as long as the pipeline includes multiple partners both within and outside of the system), and a learning orientation.

Leadership Pathways—It could be argued that leadership pathways are subsumed into pipeline initiatives. When you look at graphics of various initiatives, you see different "pathways" outlined. However, the construct of leadership pathways in this book takes into account more than one final end point in the pathway (principal). It is inclusive and represents a holistic concept of leadership and the different roles currently within an organization (and, thinking adaptively, those that have not yet been created). This is not the case when pathways within the pipeline only include options that lead to a principalship position.

Leadership pathways within a district (or other educational organization) must take into account all of the different leadership roles (formal and informal) within a district. Using an ecological mindset, everyone is interconnected. If training is provided for one person on an initiative (principal), but another person that is a part of the initiative does not receive training yet is responsible for a component of the initiative (department chair), the system will not be healthy and the initiative will more than likely falter or fail completely. The idea of leadership pathways in this sense considers the multi-faceted types of leadership in a system and plans for support and development for those roles.

Lattice for School Leadership—The lattice for school leadership is a new entry into leadership development. Supovitz (2014) has coined this phrase after an examination of leadership development in England. The lattice "features a centrally developed, high quality leadership development program combined with lateral social networks . . . a system that provides clear responsibilities for multiple levels of leadership within schools, incentives for identifying and grooming leadership within schools, pathways for leadership progression, and certification for leader attainment" (Supovitz, 2014, p. 2). Essentially the lattice has "two strands"—a hierarchical Leadership Development System paired with a network of horizontally connected schools (Supovitz, 2014). This system closely mirrors this text's assertion of the need to better acknowledge the different types of leadership roles in schools. The lattice in England has a "formalization of multiple leadership positions within schools," identifies different competencies for leadership at each leadership position, and among other components incentivizes engagement in the development system (Supovitz, 2014). The lattice provides a centralized mechanism in England to develop and support different school leaders along their career stages.

Each of these approaches should be considered and examined in depth when developing or reimagining your own Leadership Development System. Your organization may choose a different way of operationalizing the approach. In the end, your system, using the Leadership Development Ecological Framework, should be responsive to the organization's needs, be adaptive to changes in education, and incorporate the constructs that best meet your organization's needs.

Leader Types and Leadership Stages

In a Leadership Development System you need to consider both leadership role type and leadership role stage. At this point in reading this book you are probably beginning to consider your own Leadership Development System in relation to your expanded understanding about leadership development and starting to think about the constructs of your own system. In any initiative, it is important to have a baseline understanding of the system before making any changes. A Leadership Development Needs Assessment can inventory the various types of leadership roles within your system. This tool is located in Chapter 9. The inventory should meet your organization's needs, but should include items such as:

- Leadership Role Title
- Leadership Role Summary
- Essential Duties

More than likely the principal and assistant principal, as well as other formal roles, will be easier to inventory than less formal roles such as teacher leaders. Most organizations have specific job descriptions for roles like a principal. However, it is also important to survey those holding the roles themselves, as well as their supervisors, to gauge how they conceptualize these roles. Other roles like department chairs and teacher leaders may not have formalized job descriptions. In this case, a working understanding needs to be created of these positions, even if they become more site specific. The system will then have a better understanding of the types of leadership positions being developed when designing the system and creating various development initiatives.

It is impossible to create a system to develop leaders if the system does not fully understand the leadership roles that are being supported (especially if some of the roles are not being supported within the system). More robust leadership systems can then craft leadership development initiatives that are specific to those job roles. Organizations using databases can create job role codes that identify the professional development initiatives for specific roles to better aid the system designers in understanding if there is duplication of training, training that actually counters other training initiatives, or gaps in training for different roles types.

Training should also take into account various leadership role stages:

- Aspiring Leader
- Emerging Leader

- New Leader
- Transitioning Leader
- Veteran Leader

Just as we provide differentiated instruction in the classroom based upon learner need, we should also provide differentiated professional learning opportunities for educational leaders based upon their own needs, which includes their stage in leadership development. A 15-year principal veteran needs very different professional learning support as compared to a second year principal. Failure to differentiate the development needs of leaders will quickly result in failed professional development initiatives. This is not to say that these two principals could not require the same training in some cases. There are many reasons why, for different development activities, they should both be involved. However, at some point there must be a recognition of the varying needs of different leaders and the necessity of providing differentiated training where needed.

Representing Your Organization's Leadership Development Path

There are any number of ways for an organization to graphically represent the leadership development approaches within a system. The organization should have a macro view of the overall system, as well as break out the different components. For example, it is important to understand from a holistic standpoint the various pathways for leadership development and progression in a system, but it is also imperative to understand how individual leader roles (teacher leaders, assistant principals, principals, etc . . .) are developed too. It is also important to have a visual as a road map and conceptual framework for the development system. For example, see the following:

- The Wallace Foundation pipeline initiative
- The United States Department of Education School Leadership Program projects
- *Building a Lattice for School Leadership: The Top-to-Bottom Rethinking of Leadership Development in England and What It Might Mean for American Education* (Supovitz, 2014).

Consider the example below shared by Dr. Leslie Hazle Bussey, Chief of Staff for the Georgia Leadership Institute for School Improvement (GLISI). GLISI has adopted a leadership development model that incorporates many components of the four types of leadership development approaches shared in this book and specifically within this chapter. This is done through a leadership team development approach. In this way, aspiring leaders are supported by current leaders and all members of the leadership team are engaged in skill development through authentic practice. This approach is also in alignment with the *communities of practice* (CoP) structure and the process of *legitimate peripheral participation* (LPP) discussed in Chapter 6.

Example from the Field

Team Development Model

We talk about effective leadership as distributed and shared, yet most leadership development programs enroll candidates on an individual basis. That is, leader candidates learn to be leaders alone. We need to be moving toward a model where leaders learn alongside their leadership teams, working on authentic problems of practice in their schools. How can we expect leaders to be successful in leading teams or sharing leadership before they practice doing so in the safe space of a training program with expert coaching to guide their growth? As a bonus feature, a team development model also grows leadership in teachers, making the leadership work that much less lonely and that much more consistent with what research tells us works.

Dr. Leslie Hazle Bussey, Chief of Staff for the Georgia Leadership Institute for School Improvement

---

This model is further expanded upon in Chapter 9.

There are a multitude of possibilities when considering pathways for leadership development. Educational organizations need to identify their specific approaches to development and articulate the various pathways through which aspiring and current leaders can be prepared to meet the demands of the role of school leader. Crafting a system requires consideration of many factors, including defining who the leaders are within a system, the scale and scope of the system the organization is developing, and how leaders should be developed within the system. The system requires an organization to fully understand its philosophical approach to preparing leaders and to define each role within the system.

4 | Partnering for Success

A critical feature in a robust and high-quality Leadership Development System is the use of strategic and well-crafted partnerships with other organizations. According to King (2014, p. 6), "[r]esearch on exemplary school leadership preparation programs suggests that programs are more effective when school districts and training providers work together to improve principal performance." Leadership development initiatives are not feasible without different partnerships along the way. In using the Leadership Development Ecological Framework, we understand that educational organizations are not bounded and closed systems, but rather open, and there are a number of possible opportunities to capitalize on through effective partnerships. Capacity is increased through strategic and intentionally designed partnerships. The ecological framework acknowledges that schools are open systems, impacted by outside factors, that interact with each other.

Partnering with organizations allows for the cycling of resources beyond the organization itself. The use of partnerships for leadership development initiatives is not new, but it has become a popular vehicle in recent years to support leadership development across the United States. "The Danforth Foundation pioneered the concept of the university–district partnership through its Danforth Programs for the Preparation of School Principals initiative begun in the late 1980s" (Browne-Ferrigno & Muth, 2006, p. 210). Since that time a number of collaborations between universities and districts have emerged.

Partnerships between districts and universities can be very productive. Many universities have been theory-laden in the past, without a channel for authentic application of theory in the real-world setting. Districts working with universities, whether through aspiring leadership programs or with emerging and current leaders, can better help leaders understand the application of theory in real situations. "Through [a] shared commitment across institutional boundaries, the theory–practice integration of school leadership is strengthened" (Belle & Sanzo, 2014, p. 215). University faculty bring their research experiences and backgrounds to the partnership table when working with districts, as well as a potential wealth of resources for use in development activities. "In thriving collaborations, university professors provide a leadership knowledge base and assist with character refinement toward effective school leadership, while practicing administrators guide the socialization of candidates into the community of principal practice during mentored internships" (Belle & Sanzo, 2014, p. 215).

Long-standing national groups such as the National Association for Secondary School Principals and ASCD, as well as their state-level counterparts, frequently partner with school districts to provide varying levels of development and support in different initiatives. In addition, many of the reconstituted university-based leadership programs in multiple states across the US had state mandated legislation requiring partnerships with school districts in order to operate. Several leadership development organizations in the US have crafted their own development models that are not based in universities. These organizations have partnered with a number of school districts to engage in development work, sometimes in tandem with universities and at other times on their own. These organizations include the New York City Leadership Academy, the National Institute for School Leadership, and New Leaders. These different avenues for enrichment in the development process should be explored by organizations as they craft their own system.

At the national level, the United States Department of Education (USDE) has also highlighted the critical nature of partnerships in the preparation and development of school leaders. The USDE has funded over 100 multi-million dollar, multi-year leadership development projects since 2002, with one of the hallmark features being the requirement of partnerships in order to actualize the initiative. These grant-funded initiatives are a rich resource to better understand how to collaborate with multiple partners to create a robust leadership development infrastructure. "Both school districts and program providers recognize that if properly nurtured partnerships can provide fertile soil for improving the impact of preparation and training on school leaders' performance" (King, 2014, p. 6).

Partnering for Success

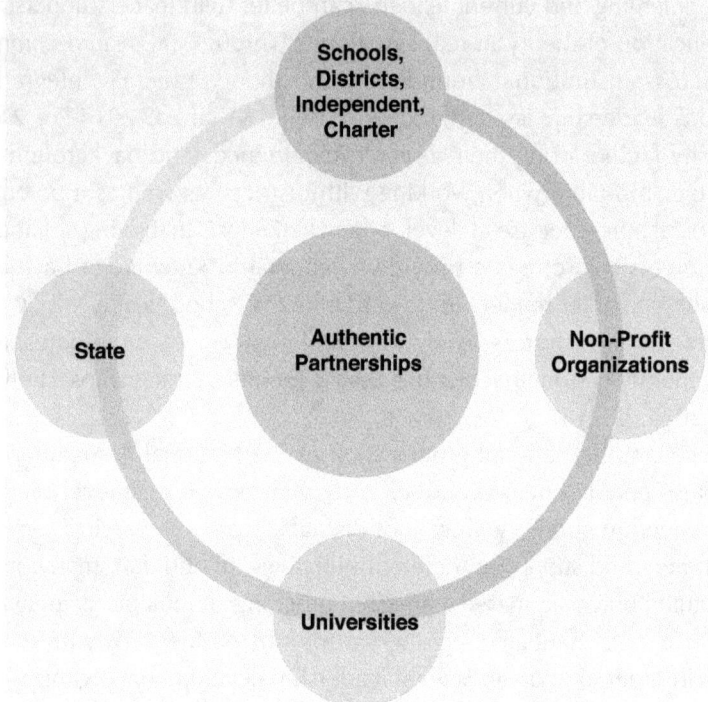

Figure 4.1 Authentic Partnership Framework
Source: Author

There are many different partnerships that educational organizations can engage in to create a Leadership Development System. These include universities, not-for-profit organizations, charter schools, public schools, independent schools, state level educational organizations, and federal level organizations. Figure 4.1 is a graphic that shows some of the various types of organizations to consider when creating an authentic partnership in your system.

Partnerships

There are a variety of ways to develop partnerships across institutions, as well as to help those partnerships be successful and sustainable. Partnerships must be formed around a core purpose and that purpose must be fully articulated. The Leadership Development System's Theory of Action will help partners understand the overarching goal(s) of the development system and to better craft meaningful partnerships around that theory.

The Leadership Development Needs Assessment Tool located in Chapter 9 is a good resource for identifying current and potential partners. This will enable the organization to review a detailed list of current partners involved in initiatives outside of the system related to leadership development, as well as potential partners. The challenge with utilizing this tool is that you must have an awareness of all initiatives in place to develop leaders. A needs assessment takes time and has to be conducted across the system in order to accurately capture the current status of efforts.

Planning for the development partnership is crucial. A criticism of leadership development partnerships between districts and other organization revolves around "flawed planning, implementation, and evaluation processes" (Miller & Hafner, 2008, p. 69). You need a framework for your approach to planning, just as you need a framework for developing the overarching Leadership Development System, to counteract potential concerns around flaws in the planning efforts. Leadership Development System designers also need to understand what effective partnerships look like and the key components for sustaining the initiative. Finally, there needs to be a mechanism to continually assess the partnership (feedback loops). The following sections will expand upon these three areas.

Planning the Partnership

Planning is important for partnership development. This book takes a collaborative planning model approach to developing and planning for authentic leadership development partnerships (Mast, Scribner, & Sanzo, 2011). This form of planning is in alignment with the Leadership Development Ecological Framework. Taking an ecological approach to planning efforts requires moving beyond a traditional planning model of sequential, lock-step processes. Ecosystems are not always predictable and can be messy, just like a collaborative planning model that "sees the nature of the world as more like an organism" (Mast, Scribner, & Sanzo, 2011, p. 33). "Collaborative planning adheres to the idea of complex adaptive systems" (Mast, Scribner, & Sanzo, 2011, p. 33) and these systems are characterized by "fragmentation, uncertainty, and complexity" (Innes & Booher, 2003, p. 10).

Table 4.1 Collaborative Planning Framework

Multiple viewpoints are involved in the planning	Stakeholders should include district leaders involved in leading professional development, coordinating professional learning for leaders, central office cabinet members (i.e., superintendent, central office leadership), building level leaders, community leaders, mentors, and coaches.
The process is values driven	The planning process involves an early process around stakeholder values identification. Values of everyone are taken into consideration, giving an opportunity for more marginalized voices to communicate their values and contribute to the planning effort.
The planning process for the partnership discourages compartmentalization of efforts	The focus of the planning effort is on collaboration and decentralizing the planning process. There should be multiple opportunities for stakeholders to be involved in the planning effort, which should be an iterative process. In this way it can be ensured that initiatives are interconnected and not duplicated, and take on a learning orientation.
There is a focus on consensus making	Group norms are agreed upon, leading to a consensus-making process for the planning effort for the partnership, rather than a majority-rules approach.
There is an acknowledgment of difference(s) in power	Most planning efforts involve the work by a few to be more intense than that of others. In addition, the investment in initiatives may demand more from one or more partners than others. This will not diminish or overly emphasize one partner over another, but acknowledges the differences in time and energy put forth by some involved in the planning effort.

The Collaborative Planning Framework, adapted from Mast, Scribner, and Sanzo (2011), can be used as you plan out partnerships in your Leadership Development System.

Constructs of Effective Partnerships

There are benefits, as well as challenges, to partnering around leadership development efforts. While there are many resources that can point to different features of effective partnerships, this text utilizes a guide developed by Myran, Crum, and Clayton (2010) to help ensure partnerships flourish in order to support and sustain an effective Leadership Development System. This guide was informed by work through a USDE School Leadership Program grant project and has been used since as a resource for the tool described in the Evaluating the Partnership section. Leadership Development System partners can use this guide to safeguard that they are following processes that will contribute to a successful partnership. The pillars should be reviewed periodically and cross-checked with the initiatives to ensure the partners are following the guide.

The Four Pillars of Effective Leadership Development Partnerships, developed by Myran, Crum, and Clayton (2010), were designed for university–district partnerships. The concepts outlined in the guide are applicable to the partners involved in a Leadership Development System. Additionally, it is also aligned to the Leadership Development Ecological Framework. A modified guide from the original is listed below, followed by explanations of each.

Pillars of Effective Leadership Development Partnerships (adapted from Myran, Crum, & Clayton, 2010)
1. Take a Developmental Approach
    a. An Iterative and Learning Orientation
    b. Transformative Growth
2. Balance between Theory and Practice
    a. An Alternative Approach to Professional Development
    b. Integrating Partnership Activities into District Initiatives
3. The Need to Develop and Maintain an Effective Communication System

Take a Developmental Approach—Partnerships take time, as do development initiatives. The developmental approach "recognizes that new understanding takes time and deep engagement to develop into well understood and generalizable . . . practices" and that "improvement efforts will need to go through a number of developmental phases and each phase will require different types of support and encouragement" (Myran, Crum, and Clayton, 2010, p. 49).

An Iterative and Learning Orientation—Leadership development efforts require feedback loops to capitalize on lessons learned to connect back to and improve the development system. The learning orientation allows improvements of the system, rather than the development system and partnership remaining static.

Transformative Growth—A developmental mindset to the partnership acknowledges that development initiatives may take time and therefore require a long-term investment by partners. However, over time, you will see a transformative growth process resulting from the work.

Balance between Theory and Practice—Regardless of the development initiative implemented by the district, a university, or a different partner, there must be an appropriate balance between the theory learned in the development process and in practice. While current and aspiring leaders may want immediately usable "tools" to employ in practice, it is important to fully understand the theory and research behind these tools to implement them with fidelity. Professional development must also be job embedded and job relevant in order to be successful.

An Alternative Approach to Professional Development—Professional development should "have immediately actionable strategies that exemplify some key aspect of the training" (Myran, Crum, & Clayton, 2010, p. 52), should provide multiple and cyclical opportunities to refine practices learned in training and to pair these lessons learned with the lived experiences of the training participants, should provide timely feedback on the experiences with the initiative, and offer chances for leaders to engage in collaborative sharing activities around their experiences with the professional development activity.

Integrating Partnership Activities into District Initiatives—Initiatives in a Leadership Development System need to be interconnected. In this way resources are used more effectively and more efficiently. The partnership activities of the system should be dovetailed where possible with other district activities.

The Need to Develop and Maintain an Effective Communication System—Partnerships work most effectively when there is a clearly articulated open communication system. This includes identifying the individual or individuals within each partnership that will serve as lead communicators, or partnership liaisons, as well as operationalizing roles and responsibilities.

Evaluating the Partnership

Evaluating the effectiveness of existing partnerships is important to promote a sustainable and quality partnership. Currently, there are few tools available to explore the various constructs of effective partnerships. One tool, developed by the Education Development Center (King, 2014), is useful in evaluating partnerships between school districts and universities. The *Quality Measures Partnership Effectiveness Continuum* is a helpful resource to self-evaluate "an existing partnership, or to support the development of a new partnership" (King, 2014, p. 7). The continuum helps partners explore their collaboration efforts around "1) partnership vision; 2) institutional leadership; 3) joint ownership and accountability for results; 4) communication and collaboration; 5) system alignment, integration, and sustainability; and 6) response to local context" (King, 2014, p. 7).

The process for completing the tool is estimated to take about a day and should involve anyone with "decision-making authority" in the partnership. The time investment is well worth the effort to come to a mutual understanding about the status and health of the partnership.

Example from the Field

Great Leaders for Great Schools Academy Partnership

One of the challenges of developing strong, robust partnerships is the actual lack of research around effective partnerships and actual examples of working partnerships. This is not to say there are no actual effective authentic partnerships in practice; rather there is a lack of published examples for others to use as a model. Much of the literature is rich with conceptual understandings of what makes a collaborative partnership effective, but is limited in actual research-based examples that have demonstrable impacts on leaders. The partnership in this example highlights work that demonstrates how to establish an authentic partnership between institutions to develop school leaders.

The Great Leaders for Great Schools Academy is a partnership between California State Polytechnic University, Pomona

(Cal Poly), the Pomona Unified School District (PUSD), and the external evaluation firm Desertfrost Consulting Group, Inc. (DFCG). Their partnership represents the story of a strong interagency collaboration that is based on a shared vision, a willingness to challenge the status quo, mutual trust, and an enduring focus on maintaining fidelity to the principles of empirical quality (Davis, Leon, & Fultz, 2012, p. 26). The partnership, funded in part through a USDE School Leadership Program grant, focused on crafting a Leadership Development System that both identified and prepared aspiring school leaders for building leaders' roles, as well as providing post-licensure support for current administrators. Key features in the leadership development partnership include: full-time mentoring and an administrative apprenticeship for aspiring leaders, a university-originated curriculum that was contextually developed around PUSD needs, a cohort format for the leadership program, a rigorous process for the selection of cohort members, a program assessment that involved multiple assessments and a feedback process to continually inform the program, and executive coaching for Cal Poly graduates who secured administrative positions with PUSD.

The partnership requires intense collaboration in order for it to be successful. Through the lived experiences of the grant partners of this highly successful leadership development program, seven recommendations emerged to aid in ongoing collaboration across institutions (Davis, Leon, & Fultz, 2012, p. 45):

1. Ensure support and buy-in from the district (involving early discussions and meetings).
2. Identify and establish mutual needs and interest (understanding that timing makes a difference in these conversations, there is a need to discern the motivation of potential partners, and an iterative and respectful process is necessary to develop the system and the evaluation process).
3. A professional external evaluator should be involved from the beginning of the design.
4. Reaffirm program goals among partners early and revisit often.
5. Anchor the system in the actual issues of schools and districts.

6. Ground program implementation strategies upon district goals and objectives.
7. Use evaluation evidence to inform system refinements and district planning.

Further, the directors of the Great Leaders for Great Schools Academy identified several considerations for engaging in a partnership. These are: (a) the willingness to listen to others with an open mind, (b) the identification of mutual needs and interest, (c) personal and professional respect, (d) patience and a degree of tolerance for ambiguity, and (e) credibility gained through personal investment and follow through (Davis, Leon, & Fultz, 2012, p. 40).

There are so many ingredients to the development of a productive and mutually supporting partnership that it's hard to zero in on one or two ideas. Nevertheless, we had to overcome the fact that IHE–K-12 partnerships (e.g., outside of teacher ed) are typically not part of the "DNA" of either institution. The licensing of educational administrators has traditionally been left to graduate schools, while the "professional" preparation of administrators occurs on the job and under the employing school district's supervision. In most cases, neither entity has had much use for the other (e.g, "we teach 'em, you hire 'em").

When we first introduced the idea of an SLP funded credentialing program partnership with the Pomona Unified School District we were met with polite (but mild) interest tempered by a large dose of skepticism. We were seen as academics who preferred the intellectual "ether" of the Ivory Tower to the "scut work" of the real world of public schools. District administrators also had a history of "hit and run" relationships with university professors who, once a grant funding period concluded, left the district in the lurch while they published their findings and moved on to new projects. The GLGSA grant proposal was a nice idea in theory, but our soon-to-be school district partner was wary of the university in terms of what it could add that would be of real value to the day-to-day demands of running a school district. In addition, the district had yet to buy into the theory that robust IHE–K-12 partnerships and collaborations would result in better prepared new administrators. As former school district administrators, the university faculty team leading the GLGSA project understood the challenges and knew that we had to "sell" the idea (tactfully and strategically). We began by climbing down from the Ivory Tower. We spent hours and hours with the district, talking to principals, district administrators, and scheduling meetings on the district's "turf." We were patient. Although we had a short timeline to craft and submit an SLP grant proposal, we knew that it would take many more months of meetings, conversations, and collaborative planning before we could hope to bring our partner district "on-board." Most important, we had to create a program that met the district's leadership and student needs, the state's credentialing requirements, and involved the direct participation of key district department leaders. In essence, we had to give a little to get a lot.

It took three years before our district partner fully bought into the value-added dynamic of a mutually engaged partnership. The proof, as they say, was in the pudding. GLGSA graduates began to apply for district administrative positions, AND were hired with increasing frequency. Moreover, their performance on the job impressed district officials—and the rest is history.

Now, at the twilight of the SLP grant funding period, our partner district has come full circle in terms of embracing the concept of strong interagency partnerships, and most importantly the idea that it is in a school district's best interests to build its internal capacity to identify, cultivate, select, train, and evaluate school leaders. One thing is certain, without deep and enduring partnerships with K-12 districts, administrator credential programs will continue to provide "hit or miss" preparation experiences to prospective school leaders.

Dr. Stephen Davis, Director of the Great Leaders for Great Schools Grant, describes his experience working with a school district as a university faculty member on an intensive leadership development partnership, his personal reflections on the project, and advice for the field on leadership development partnerships in general.

Partnering with a High-Quality Leadership Program

There are a number of factors to contemplate when considering one or more leadership program partnerships. While traditionally these preparation partnerships have been with university-based leadership programs, there are several national programs that are becoming popular, including New Leaders, the New York City Leadership Academy, and TNTP. Regardless of organizational affiliation, program quality is paramount. The first consideration should always be if the state recognizes the program as an approved pathway for leadership licensure. Otherwise, that partnership, more than likely, would not be a viable option for preparing aspiring school leaders for a Leadership Development System.

Researchers have explored the various facets that are a part of high-quality Leadership Development Systems. Within the past 10 to 15 years, program components have been coupled in a positive light with the term "innovative." What is considered innovative currently can be questionable, given that many programs have transformed their approaches to leadership development within that same time frame because of the heightened level of scrutiny on leadership preparation. Novel should not be confused for innovative and sustainable. As programs are being considered, unique program features should be carefully examined for their viability with the Leadership Development System and sustainability. If a program feature is interesting and novel, but not realistic, then the likelihood would be low that the program will be as successful as the system designers had anticipated. The following program features have been recognized as contributing to a high-quality leadership development program:

Problem-Based Learning—The use of problem-based learning tools, including case studies and simulations, are found throughout the literature to help promote adult learning. These practical, "real-life" activities help to simulate different leadership situations through scenario development that aspiring and current leaders may encounter. More specific information on simulations is provided in Chapter 8. According to Jackson and Kelly (2002, p. 196), "PBL centers on professional problems, so that students develop and bring a variety of resources (such as research, data, and prior experiences) to the clarification and resolution of professional problems."

Cohorts—The use of cohorts in leadership preparation is common (Jackson & Kelly, 2002). In a brief synthesis of cohort literature, Jackson and Kelly noted that cohorts help promote professional networks both within and across groups, allow for a more coherent programmatic sequence and structure, and promote personal relationships within the cohorts. A US Department of Education Office of Innovation and Improvement study (2004) found in a review of innovative leadership preparation programs that "all programs use a cohort structure and all report that participants find cohort interactions to be the most valuable element of the program. Cohorts allow participants to proceed through the program with the safety and support of a learning community" (p. 20). More details on cohorts are provided in Chapter 8.

Collaborative Partnerships—As evidenced by this chapter, partnerships are important in a Leadership Development System. Davis et al. (2005) highlighted "strong partnerships with schools and districts to support quality field-based learning" (p. 25) in their study on principal preparation programs. The US Department of Education Office of Innovation and Improvement (2004) study also found that "all of the programs studied operate as partnerships between a school district or multiple school jurisdictions and other entities, notably universities and foundations. Such partnerships often support the initial costs of program staffing, design, and development, and they contribute to the program's long-term sustainability" (p. 16).

Field Experiences—According to Jackson and Kelly (2002, p. 197), "Researchers examining cognitive approaches to leadership preparation suggest that field experiences should provide core learning experiences in programs to enable future leaders to observe, participate in, and dissect important cognitive processes associated with identifying and addressing problems in the leadership and management of organizations." More details on field-based experiences are provided in Chapter 8.

Partnerships are instrumental in the success of a cohesive Leadership Development System. No one organization can effectively meet the development needs of a system internally. There are multiple preparation initiatives that must occur within a system. Partnerships enable organizations both to capitalize on their own internal capacity and to tap into external resources to enhance the system. Any partnership must have at its foundation an understanding of the purpose of the partnership, an agreement about the communication process employed in the partnership, the roles and responsibilities of the partners, and the pillars of effective partnerships.

5 | Grow-Your-Own Model
Aspiring Leaders

There is a very real urgency to immediately address how to reinvent Leadership Development Systems to improve education. It is no longer the case that districts can sit back and wait for their staff to complete a leadership credentialing program at any university and expect to have a pool of high-quality school leaders ready to take on various administrative roles, or expect that current leaders are able to receive the appropriate professional development by only attending external conferences outside of the system.

Districts are taking control of their leadership development initiatives. This book advocates for a comprehensive Leadership Development System that is crafted for and by the organization and with a host of partners involved in the development of leaders. This should start not with your current school leaders, but with those who are aspiring leaders and possess the potential to transition into leadership roles.

Aspiring and Emerging Leaders

Districts should cultivate exceptional talent from within and develop a model where they themselves can "grow their own" leaders, rather than waiting for their employees to take the initiative on their own. Those individuals who seek out opportunities to earn their leadership credentials outside of a partnership situation with the district should be included in the Leadership Development System. However, educational organizations should understand the leadership preparation program, the competencies required by the program, the developmental activities, and the practical/

hands-on training provided to aspiring leaders. Your organization may choose to research each program to learn about how they prepare aspiring leaders, or develop more formal relationships and partnerships with leadership development programs to better meet the needs of the organization. It is important not to exclude educators from outside the district when considering who is the right fit for the district and a leadership position. There is value in bringing in outside voices, ideas, and experiences into the leadership system.

Rather than waiting for staff to earn their own leadership endorsements through university-based programs and obtain their initial leadership training through an outside source, many districts are collaborating with university preparation programs and other non-university-based entities to tailor-design a leadership credentialing program that will prepare educators to meet the unique demands of the district. Proactively creating a path for leadership development and credentialing for staff will prove successful for the district when done well. This was illustrated in several of the previous examples in this book, including the Great Leaders for Great Schools Academy partnership with Cal Poly Pomona and the Pomona Unified School District. Below is an example of a district–university partnership to prepare aspiring school leaders.

Example from the Field

Alliance for Leading and Learning (ALL)

The ALL program is a leadership preparation partnership between Albuquerque Public Schools in New Mexico and the University of New Mexico.

Aspiring principal participants report that the Alliance for Leading and Learning project's co-taught administrator licensure courses with a University of New Mexico (UNM) faculty member and an Albuquerque Public School (APS) principal prepared them for their internship experience, making the model a program strength in the preparation of aspiring principals. Both aspiring principals and instructors continuously speak to the benefits of the model and

Grow-Your-Own Model: Aspiring Leaders

> its ability to offer experiences that bridge the gap between theory and practice.
>
> Sharon Olguin, Director of the Alliance for Leading and Learning Grant and a District Mentor Principal for Albuquerque Public Schools, shares her view of the partnership between APS and a university leadership program.

These models can be firmly situated within an overarching Leadership Development System and, in fact, can be one of the expressed purposes of the system. There is a strong desire by districts to cultivate leadership talent from within. There is no reason to wait for staff to seek out leadership credentialing opportunities on their own. While self-motivation to obtain a leadership degree and credential is admirable, it is not always the case that the leadership credentialing institution's program is tailored to meet the specific demands of your own system. Each district should take time to understand the curriculum of each school leadership credentialing institution from which the potential pool of school leaders comes, the philosophical approach to preparation in the institutions, and how the institutions prepare candidates (for example, activities, delivery modal, and field-based experiences). Partnering with these institutions allows districts to better direct the focus of the curriculum and ensure it is being dovetailed with the contextual needs of the district.

It is easier for larger districts to develop relationships with credentialing institutions such as a university leadership preparation program to create their own individual grow-your-own program for aspiring leaders. The number of teachers on staff in a mid-sized urban district typically allows for at least one to two cohorts of aspiring leaders per year or two as part of a comprehensive Leadership Development System. Large urban districts can sustain several aspiring leadership cohorts each year. However, smaller districts that do not have enough personnel to go through a leadership program can create a consortium and partner with a university or other credentialing organization to develop their own "grow-your-own model." Below is an example of one such consortium.

> *Example from the Field*
>
> ### Northeastern North Carolina School Leadership Program (NNCSLP)
>
> Nine high-need rural school districts (Bertie, Chowan, Edgecombe, Halifax-Weldon City, Northampton, Pasquotank, Perquimans, Warren, and Washington in North Carolina) developed a consortium to address, among other topics, leadership development. The districts were smaller and did not have the internal capacity to create the type of robust Leadership Development System they knew was important to cultivate high-quality leaders. In this way they recognized the open system nature of their districts and the power of cycling resources. Using their learning orientation, they contacted a university partner (Elizabeth City State University) and through their collaborative efforts a consortium was developed. Through the consortium the Northeastern North Carolina School Program was created. In addition, the consortium was able to use its collective resources to craft a competitive grant application to invest much needed money into the development program through the USDE School Leadership Program.
>
> By capitalizing on the open system concept through an ecological approach to leadership development, the nine districts and the university are able to collaborate to prepare outstanding leaders in their districts. The grow-your-own program incorporates state level standards and models into the program. Grounded on the idea that job-embedded professional development is connected to an increase in student achievement, the program utilizes a variety of activities to prepare school leaders. These collaboratively developed and implemented activities include summer institutes, mentoring, and seminars.

Aspiring Leadership Development

The aspiring leadership component of a Leadership Development System must take into account several factors:

- **Is your organization large enough to develop your own aspiring leadership system?**

  As discussed previously, smaller districts can collaborate to create a healthy Leadership Development System that is mutually beneficial for all institutions involved. Larger districts generally have enough aspiring leaders without leadership credentials to partner with development providers. The question arises in this case as to the benefit of creating a partnership on your own or partnering with another district (or multiple districts). While there is always the concern that a broader consortium of districts may cause some employees to leave one system and join another, over the long term this type of collaborative system can help develop leaders to meet the demands of varied systems and to be better equipped to serve schools and students. Multiple partners bring in multiple experiences and perspectives, more resources, and can help to promote a learning orientation.

- **Who are the credentialing institutions available to partner with?**

  Generally there are at least several options for districts to consider when seeking out a partnership to prepare the next generation of leaders in a district. Brick and mortar campuses are not constrained to a small driving radius to serve the needs of district partners. Distance technology, satellite campuses, and innovative approaches to leadership development allow districts more freedom in the choice of partners. Additionally, in some states there are non-university-based options to secure a leadership credential. Ultimately, program quality and program fit with the district Leadership Development System need to be primary drivers in selecting a program to partnership with in the development initiative. Later in this chapter the characteristics of high-quality leadership preparation programs will be reviewed. It can be the case that a district would want to partner with multiple leadership credentialing partners to give their aspiring leaders a wider choice of options when seeking licensure. The Principal Pipeline Initiative, for example, in Charlotte-Mecklenburg Schools provides four different routes for aspiring leadership preparation.

- **What is the outcome of your Leadership Development Needs Assessment?**

  Results from the Leadership Development Needs Assessment Tool (see Chapter 9) should be a factor in the decision-making process around

Grow-Your-Own Model: Aspiring Leaders

the design of the aspiring leadership program. This assessment can help you factor in previous and current development initiatives, current and potential partners, as well as resources available in the design of the system.

- **Who are the aspiring leaders in your system?**

    Some aspiring leaders in your district may already hold a leadership endorsement, while others may be seeking out ways to earn their endorsements. The system you develop should factor in both populations.

Types of Aspiring Leaders

The Leadership Development System in a grow-your-own model needs to incorporate three different types of aspiring leaders (see Figure 5.1). As the staff members progress through the Leadership Development System, they transition from aspiring leaders, to aspiring leaders in training, to a talent pool consisting of qualified leaders for the school system.

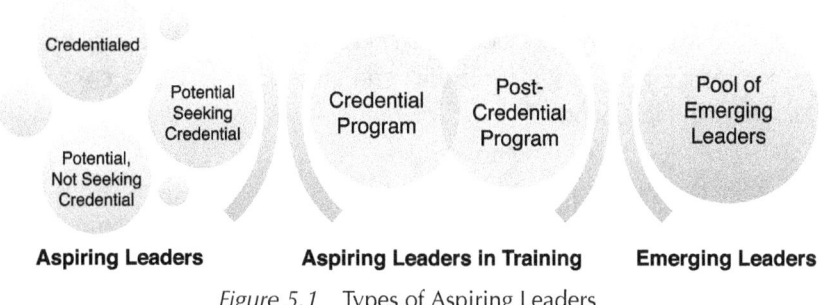

Figure 5.1   Types of Aspiring Leaders
Source: Author

Aspiring Leaders

- Credentialed Staff: Credentialed staff members already hold a leadership endorsement from a state agency that credentials this person to serve in leadership roles. These staff members have already gone through a formal university or other credentialing program, but need to continue to engage in school district specific training initiatives in order to better develop and hone their leadership skills to match the needs of the system.

- Potential Seeking Credential: Staff members with leadership potential who do not yet have their leadership credentials need to participate in a program that will lead to a leadership endorsement for the state or within the educational organization. These are staff members that already possess the intrinsic desire to transition into a leadership position.
- Potential, Not Seeking Credential: Often school administrators recognize leadership potential in staff members before those staff members believe in their own abilities to serve in a leadership position. These individuals need to have ongoing support and encouragement to seek out leadership opportunities and consider transitioning into leadership positions.

Creating a Dual Track Aspiring Leader in Training System

Consideration needs to be given, as highlighted previously, to those interested in obtaining a leadership credential, those with potential but not yet interested in seeking a credential, and those already with a credential. As addressed in Chapter 3, there are different types of leaders to consider when crafting a development system.

Throughout this book there are a variety of suggestions, tools, and activities to engage staff in the leadership development continuum. It is highly recommended that while using these different strategies, as well as those of your own, districts provide the opportunity for all aspiring leaders in training to engage in common development activities.

Common training experiences to consider are:

- weekend training sessions
- webinars
- field-based projects
- leadership institutes
- coaching seminars.

The Leadership Development Ecological Framework highlights the need to cycle resources and consider the interconnectedness of organizations. In this way, Leadership Development Systems need to maximize internal capacity. It is important for those coordinating the various initiatives within an overarching system to communicate with one another about ongoing opportunities. For example, if the Post-Credential Program has invited a national speaker to work with the staff, those in the Credential Program should be invited to participate. This allows resources to be maximized, as well as for a continuity of experiences across leadership personnel in the system.

Recruitment and Selection

"[S]election is a touchstone for judging a program's purposes and assumptions about leadership" (Orr, 2006, p. 494). It is important to create a robust system that identifies teachers and other staff members with leadership potential and grooms them for leadership positions. "Effective recruitment and selection of school administrators continue to be one of the more challenging human resource tasks in educational organization" (Normore, 2004, p. 3). Those practices must focus on the recruitment of potential leaders, as well as on ways to retain qualified candidates (and leaders) once they have been recruited and selected (Castetter & Young, 2000). This section on recruitment and selection is directed specifically at the identification of aspiring leaders for a credentialing program that is a partnership with a district (or districts) and part of a broader Leadership Development System. Aspects of the recruitment and selection process can be applied to other components of the Leadership Development System, for example aspiring leaders with credentials going into a pre-leadership training program or principals applying to be part of a cadre of Principal Fellows in your district. There are many different ways to selectively recruit and identify aspiring leaders to enter into a program.

The New York City Leadership Academy (NYCLA) was developed by the New York City Department of Education as a "grow-your-own" model to develop school principals. Recruitment and selection is critical in NYCLA. The selection process is an important part of NYCLA's theory of change. While anyone can apply to NYCLA, "it relies on a network of mentor principals, former graduates, and district leaders to recruit promising candidates" (Corcoran, Schwartz, & Weinstein, 2012, p. 234). Recruitment activities, as identified by Corcoran, Schwartz, and Weinstein in 2012, included:

- information sessions
- program website
- other forms of recruitment to encourage a diverse candidate pool.

The admissions process for NYCLA, as cited by the 2012 report, is conducted in three stages (Corcoran, Schwartz, & Weinstein, 2012): written application, group interview, and individual interview. The selection process continues throughout the training program, with an average graduation rate of 81% (Corcoran, Schwartz, & Weinstein, 2012).

The following example from the field describes a recruitment and selection process drawn from practice in a PK-12 setting. Individual examples from this book and other resources can be fed directly into your own system's program, or a synthesis of components can be developed to craft your own recruitment and selection process. The best process is one that is based upon proven effective practices and developed to fit your specific context and system.

Example from the Field

Recruiting and Selecting Aspiring Leaders for a Cohort Program

The HCS–ODU partnership is a program between the Hampton City Schools district in Virginia and the educational leadership program at Old Dominion University. This program has been in existence for over a decade and involves the preparation of aspiring school leaders to meet the unique and diverse needs of the school system.

The recruitment process begins with notification:

- multiple division-wide emails
- information sessions about the program
- individual conversations with potential program candidates.

The selection process involves an application tailored to the school system, as well as an innovative interview process described below.

The Application: The application involves multiple components. There are the university-based program entrance requirements, in addition to three professional references with a tailored applicant rating form designed specifically for the school system based on district and state leadership standards, a resume, and three essays centered around the district's student learning needs and strategic priorities.

The Interview: The interview does not involve a traditional single interviewee and a panel of interviewers. Applicants participate in a two-step interview process after the initial paper screen of applicants. The interview panel consists of at least seven district personnel representing different departments at the central office, including principal supervisors and principals, and at least three university personnel from the educational leadership program. Each applicant participates in a two-hour interview. First, applicants respond individually in writing to a case study scenario provided to them at the start of the day. After a one-hour writing response session, applicants then participate in a "fish-bowl" interview exercise. Applicants are placed in groups with three to four other applicants. No applicants work together and therefore most do not know each other. Groups are mixed in order to allow different grade levels and content areas to participate in the same group. Once in the room with the interview panel, the applicants have about sixty minutes for the interview process that consists of the following:

1. Applicants discuss the case situation for fifteen minutes.
2. Applicants have fifteen minutes to devise a plan of action regarding the case situation.

    (During this time the interview panel is observing the conversation and interactions of the applicants. This allows the panel to learn about communication skills, interpersonal dynamics, leadership potential, and decision-making ability.)

> 3. Applicants present the case study response to the panel for ten minutes.
> 4. The interview panel asks probing and clarifying questions for twenty minutes.
>
> This innovative interview process has proven very successful for the partnership and has been integrated into other application processes for other cohorts with the university.

Cultivating exceptional internal leadership talent is a responsibility of the educational organization. This can and should be done in partnership with other organizations. However, districts cannot wait until there is a vacant leadership position to begin developing their own personnel. A "grow-your-own" aspiring leadership model can greatly enhance a cohesive Leadership Development System and develop exceptional leaders within a system who are ready to take on new educational roles. There are many factors to consider when crafting this component of a Leadership Development System, including the capacity of the organization to prepare aspiring and emerging leaders, the types of aspiring leaders within the system, and how to craft a dual track development system.

Grow-Your-Own Model
Current Leaders

Current school leaders need a variety of professional learning opportunities and experiences. The best school systems throughout the world invest in leadership through various support mechanisms, including aspiring school leader development and professional development for leaders (Wallace Foundation, 2013). Unfortunately, many factors, such as severe fiscal restraints, have contributed to professional development not being a high priority for current school leaders (Wallace Foundation, 2013). However, there are ways to capitalize on internal resources already in place through a Leadership Development Ecological Framework to better support current school leaders without causing severe financial hardships on districts. Additionally, there has been more funding support for leadership development in recent years as states have become more willing to provide additional investment in leadership (Wallace Foundation, 2013).

As in the case of aspiring school leaders, there are different types of current school leaders. This includes job type (assistant principal, principal, curriculum director, principal supervisor, and other roles) as well as experience level (e.g., first year assistant principal versus an assistant principal who has held the role for five years). These factors should be considered when creating a Leadership Development System.

For example, first year principals' needs are vastly different than those of ten-year principal veterans. Research demonstrates that "inexperienced principals comprise a significant percentage of school leaders" (Bastian & Henry, 2014, p. 2). Specifically, in a study looking at North Carolina, over half of all school leaders in public schools across the state had no more than four years of experience in their leadership roles (Bastian & Henry, 2014). Student achievement can be negatively impacted by leaders with little experience in their current roles (Beteille, Kalogrides, & Loeb, 2012). Given the challenges with new leaders in particular, specific support structures and processes need to be a primary goal for a Leadership Development System.

The Leadership Development Ecological Framework should be used when designing the current Leadership Development System in an organization. This framework enables professional developers to think holistically about the system, as well as consider each experience level and job type when planning the system. While the role of new leaders and their professional development needs should be a central feature of this system for current leaders, veteran school leaders must also be carefully considered in this holistic model and provided with their own set of support structures.

Developing current school leaders has traditionally been the role of school districts. Often, in the past, districts had to create their own support structures in a vacuum and with few resources. Luckily, today there are many opportunities for districts and other organizations to partner with one another. Potential partners include both universities and other organizations that engage in leadership development work.

Professional Development

Professional development (PD) for current school leaders is important for many different reasons, as highlighted at the start of this chapter. Once an educator completes a leadership credentialing program, there is still much to learn regarding the specifics of the job. For example, principals need continual development around content knowledge for subjects taught in their schools in order to effectively observe and support instruction in the classrooms. "Administrative certification programs rarely focus on content knowledge in ways that teacher certification programs do" (Steele et al., 2015, p. 3). However, PD initiatives should not simply focus on individual content areas. Rather, they should be integrated—following the Leadership Development Ecological Framework. "Transformative PD moves beyond specific curriculum materials or activities toward general principles that link teaching and learning" (Steele et al., 2015, p. 4).

Professional development for leaders should focus on leveraging effective leaders and leadership practices through systematic leadership preparation experiences that will significantly and positively affect student learning. One way of approaching professional development through an integrative manner, utilizing the Leadership Development Ecological Framework, is to work within a *communities of practice* (CoPs) structure, specifically through the process of *legitimate peripheral participation* (LPP) (Lave & Wenger, 1991). LPP guides us in terms of how to bring novice educational leaders from the periphery of their new profession into the center as an expert practitioner. An effective system utilizing LPP moves aspiring leaders toward mastery of their new role as emergent educational leaders and provides activities through which current principals interact and engage with new knowledge and people to deepen their expertise, sharpen their identity as educational leaders, and increase their commitment to their CoP.

Aspiring school leaders remain on the periphery while they acquire and assimilate various types of procedural and propositional knowledge, and then develop their own professional repertoire through the prism of practice (Eraut, 1994). Novice and experienced leaders should engage in socializing experiences that will bring new leaders into the field with specific knowledge, skills, and dispositions, and revitalize current principals with refreshed and new knowledge and experiences. Further, through school improvement practices, leaders will at once learn the skills of school improvement while also leading, teaching, and forming new CoPs within their schools. Practicing principals can deepen their knowledge and further develop skills related to coaching, culture and community building, group facilitation of data-based discussion, and related topics (Darling-Hammond, 2010; Darling-Hammond et al., 2009).

Strong professional communities have more engaged learning environments and better student achievement than schools with weaker professional communities (e.g., Rosenholtz, 1991; Scribner et al., 1999; Seashore Louis, Marks, & Kruse, 1996). Rigorous research has shown school environments in which teachers and leaders 1) share certain norms and values around student learning, 2) collaborate around vexing problems of practice, 3) focus on student and teacher data, 4) observe others' teaching practices, and 5) engage in reflective dialogues that tend to produce greater student learning results than schools that do not possess these attributes (see, for example, Goddard, Goddard, & Tschannen-Moran, 2007; Newman & Associates, 1997; Seashore Louis, Marks, & Kruse, 1996; Supovitz & Christman, 2003).

What Does PD Look Like for Current Leaders?

There are many different ways to support leadership development in schools and districts. The specific development system should be based on a comprehensive needs assessment of current and anticipated future leadership support needs. However, there are a variety of strategies you can consider when developing your system. For example:

- New principals in New York City are provided with individualized coaching support throughout their first year. Using a diagnostic tool to support the coaching, principals are engaged with their leadership coach for an average of 72 hours during that first year (Wallace Foundation).
- Many school districts engage in summer leadership conferences. In Hampton City Schools, Virginia, school leaders are using a Consultancy Protocol in their summer conference to guide their critical conversations around school learning plans. This embedded PD not only provides them with role-alike structured conversations to deeply examine their learning data, but also provides a structured process for the leaders to take back to their own work settings and use as a tool with their school-based communities of practice.
- In the Mississippi Leadership Excellence for Acceleration in Developing Schools Program participating school leaders take part in "action projects" while on the job. These projects are paired with professional development where the leaders are able to apply the knowledge gained through their development activities to better learn about real problems within their contextual setting. These situated learning activities allow them to better understand their own problems of practice through contextualized experiences.
- In Saint Paul, Minnesota, school leaders in the 2010–2015 Turnaround Saint Paul USDE School Leadership Program grant engaged in a variety of professional development opportunities. The focus of these support activities was to increase the instructional leadership capacity of principals and included: formal leadership development sessions, professional learning community networking, and coaching. Formal leadership development sessions were spread out through the course of each year (six to eight sessions) and included topics such as analyzing data and data use, instructional engagement and improvement, and forming community partnerships.

- Principal and Assistant Principal teams in the Learning-Centered Leadership Development Program participated in ongoing training throughout the course of the five-year grant. This collaborative partnership program between Western Michigan University and a consortium of twelve school districts in Michigan involved learning activities, mentoring, and online activities. Delving more deeply into the learning activities component, the four learning activities for the participants were:
    (a) participation of each principal "in a two-and-a-half day workshop for each of the seven dimensions of principal leadership (each workshop is a distinct module focusing on one leadership dimension)";
    (b) each leadership pair (Assistant Principal and Principal) worked with a mentor and school stakeholders to "examine the practice of that leadership dimension in the school" to develop "at least one renewal activity related to each domain";
    (c) implementation of at least one renewal activity per module by the Assistant Principal/Principal team; and
    (d) participating in a project sharing process with program participants, mentors, and stakeholders through online and in person activities. (Western Michigan University, 2010, p. 12).

More tools and resources from the Learning-Centered Leadership Development Program are provided in Chapter 9.

The following four examples from the field feature additional types of professional development opportunities for current school leaders.

Example from the Field

Communities of Practice to Develop Leaders

We have emerged from the time of educational management to instructional leadership. In order to have a true collaborative learning culture focused on learning, we have to embrace feedback and continuous growth. One of the ways that we have accomplished this is by developing instructional leaders and coaches within our building. Three years ago, we started from scratch and everyone had their own understanding of what "good" instruction looked like. Now we are a much more cohesive group with a common understanding of high-quality instruction and teachers are provided with frequent and consistent feedback while also giving them support before, during, and after instruction to improve. Below is a brief description of how we did it.

In the first year, we shifted the role of assistant principals and developed their capacity to see learning taking place in classrooms on a frequent basis. We calibrated our instructional lens through group observations followed up by group conversations about what we saw and the conversation that we would like to have with the teacher. We were all over the place at first but slowly came in line with a consistent understanding. The calibration piece is critical and we continue to schedule four full days per year for group calibration observations. We also meet every two weeks as an instructional administrative team to talk about the 6–10 observations that each person has conducted over the past two weeks, the high and low points, and most importantly the instructional conversation with the teacher. Administrators pair up for at least one observation every two weeks to ensure that there is consistency and continued calibration among all administrators. During the first year, we also purchased the book *Mindset* by Carol Dweck for all staff. Staff were not required to read the text, but it started the conversation and several follow up small group sessions were held to discuss the key concepts and implications for our work.

In year two, we continued our work with administrators but then brought in several other key instructional leaders to the conversation. These included the gifted resource teacher, reading specialist, and a math teacher that was given two instructional blocks off for instructional coaching. These leaders were provided with the same training and support as our administrators and they observed with administrators to calibrate their instructional lens. The goal was to ensure that we were providing all teachers with consistent feedback about their instruction regardless of the observer. We were very careful to reinforce that the process was formative in nature and not evaluative and we started observing teachers that sought out opportunities to improve their instruction. The instructional leaders that were brought on board in year two worked alongside teachers to plan, model, and assess instructional practices while developing the capacity of each teacher to implement these processes on their own without the daily support of the instructional leader.

The third year offered opportunities to expand our work and to reach more teachers. We included our instructional technology specialists, library media specialists, and a majority of our department chairs, who were willing to take on the responsibility as instructional leaders. Ongoing training and calibration were provided through the summer and during our instructional leadership team meetings. Each of our instructional leaders was involved in several different collaborative planning groups with teachers where they could provide coaching and feedback during the planning process as well as through classroom observations. Department chairs were asked to observe and give feedback to each teacher in their department at least once per year and collaboratively review learning plans for each teacher once per semester. Learning walks were conducted with small groups of instructional leaders throughout the year to calibrate and provide ongoing support. We also continued to reinforce the focus on formative feedback and continuous improvement.

Currently, as a result of our work to develop a collaborative learning culture, we are seeing positive results across the board. Test scores and graduation rates are up and discipline rates are down. More and more of our teachers and staff are embracing feedback and they want to continue to improve.

> Dr. Daniel Smith, Principal at Princess Anne High School in Virginia Beach City Public Schools, Virginia, shares above the practical application of the CoP and LPP concept within his district.

Example from the Field

A Leadership Philosophy in Action with New Leaders

Leadership is not a solo act. Ensuring that those who have a stake in the outcomes of specific decisions are invited to share in the decision-making process is vital (see Figure 6.1). The leader must learn to listen to those he or she is leading, taking into account their ideas and expertise. True leadership is the facilitation of meshing together ideas with a laser focus on a single vision.

The most effective leaders are able to leverage their influence with the motivation of moving toward a single vision. The secret to wielding influence effectively is through building positive relationships with those they are leading. Once trust is established and credibility is garnered, then a leader can guide others through the decision-making process—helping others to maintain focus on a shared goal or common vision. I assist new leaders in this process through discussions around the importance of listening and securing quick wins. This is essential in the beginning of relationships. Following through on the small things assures quick wins and builds credibility, which in turn strengthens the relationships between the leader and those she is leading.

Dr. Christy Teal, Assistant Superintendent for Human Resources in Carroll County Schools, Georgia, shares her leadership philosophy and how she works with new leaders to help them understand and incorporate this philosophy into their work.

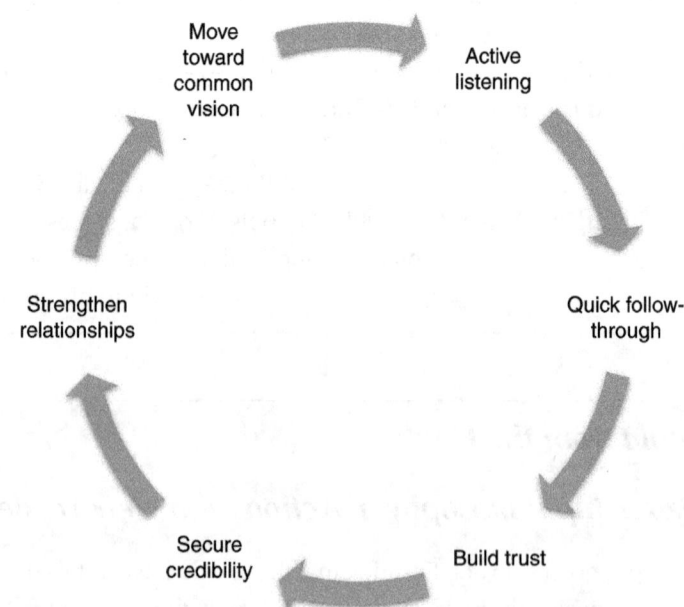

Figure 6.1 Leadership Philosophy—Christy Teal
Source: © Christy Teal. Used with permission.

Example from the Field

The National School Administration Manager Innovation Project

The National School Administration Manager (SAM) Innovation Project was developed by the Wallace Foundation in 2002. The original pilot project has expanded into a nationwide initiative by Wallace to help principals focus on instructional leadership activities with the expressed purpose of enhancing both teaching and student learning. The SAM process involves: collecting data on how a principal currently spends his or her time; training others who can respond to questions and protect the principal's time; use of a cloud-based calendar system, TimeTrack™; and on-site training and coaching for principals and staff focused on strengthening principals' ability to promote high-quality teaching (Wallace Foundation, n.d.). Access more information at: www.wallacefoundation.org/Pages/SAM.aspx

The *National SAM Innovation Project* has been a transformational experience for me. In my previous administrative roles, I often felt fractured by the competing interests that take the building leader out of the classroom. The SAM process does not reduce the importance of the day-to-day duties or urgencies, rather it gives the building principal the freedom to delegate those things to other appropriate building leaders (First Responders as they are called under the SAM Model). This ensures that management and safety remain high priorities without distracting the principal from a commitment to instruction and student learning.

The process focuses on affecting instruction and student learning through the targeted and efficient use of the building principal's time. I begin each day with a strategic "lesson plan" driven by data. Using the TimeTrack™ calendar, I document everything I do and the program calculates and disaggregates how I allocate time among instructional and management duties. The variety of TimeTrack™ reports provide complex data that allow me to dissect, examine, monitor, and reflect on my practices—observations, coaching, informal modeling, support, research time, feedback, etc. The SAM model challenges and guides me

> to be intentional in everything I do so that I truly serve as an instructional leader.
>
> Tiffany Hardy, Principal of Instruction at Hampton High School in Hampton, Virginia, shares her transformational experiences of the professional development provided through SAM.

Example from the Field

Developing First Year Principals

The Alliance for Leading and Learning (ALL) Program in Albuquerque, New Mexico, was created to provide a comprehensive Leadership Development System to support school leaders. The program provides development and support for aspiring and current school leaders. Within the overall holistic framework, the ALL program has models for each aspect of the system. Figure 6.2 shows the framework for supporting first year principals. The program involves peer mentors, a district mentor, a variety of workshops for supporting first year principals, and seminars.

Differentiated professional development is important for current school leaders. Just as there is a qualitative difference between new teachers and veteran teachers in terms of their training and preparation needs, the same holds true for school leaders. In addition, leadership role type is an important consideration when crafting professional development for school leaders in determining the type of initiatives provided. Professional development for school leaders must leverage the capacity of the educational organization and partners to craft high-quality initiatives that meet the specific needs of the organization. As demonstrated in this chapter, there are a variety of activities that can be implemented for current school leaders, and those activities and initiatives should be contextualized to the organization.

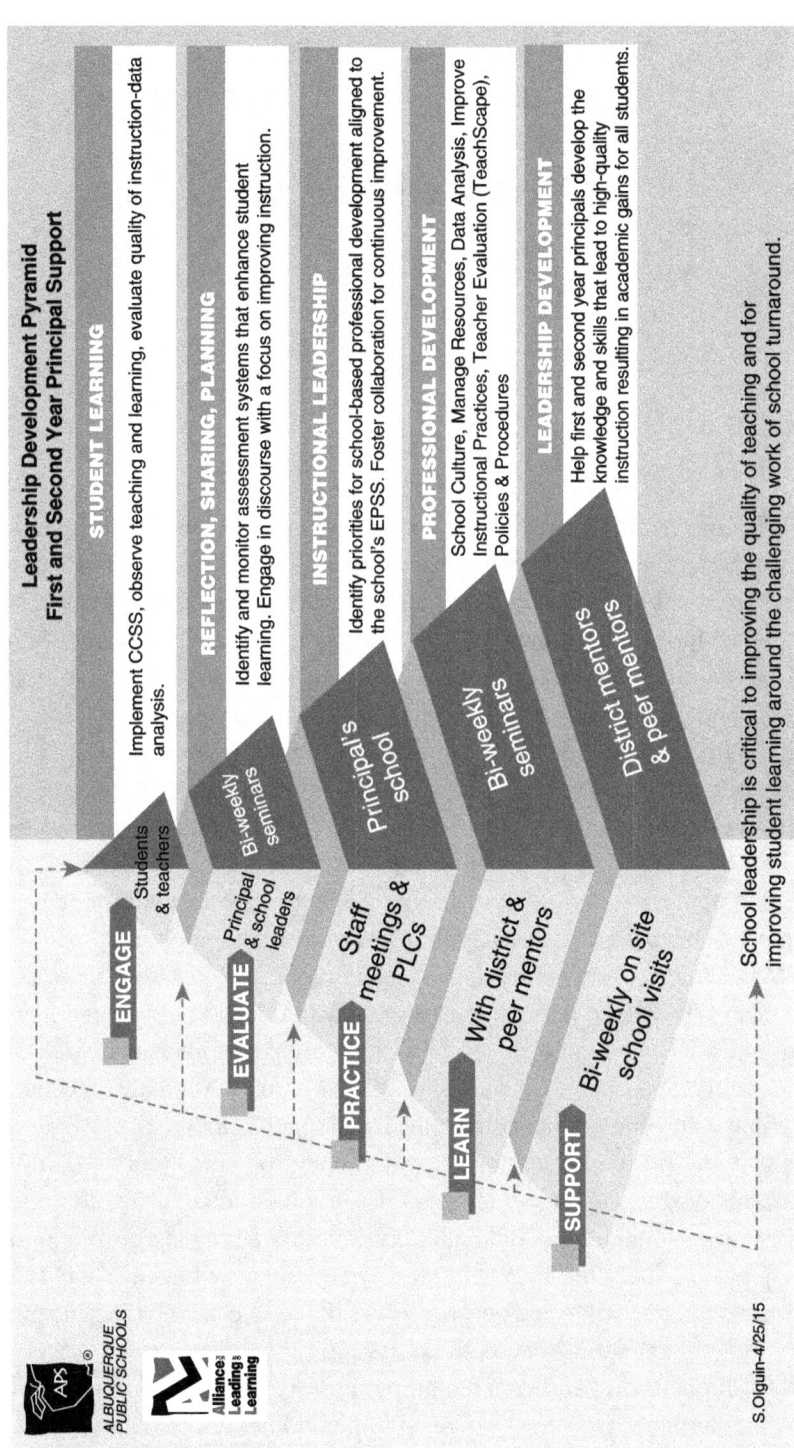

Figure 6.2 Alliance for Leading and Learning (ALL) Program First Year Leadership Development Model

Source: © Sharon Olguin. Used with permission.

7 Mentoring and Coaching

The idea of providing one-on-one support to aspiring and current school leaders is not new. Although coaching is gaining traction as a distinctive model, it is still relatively young as a concept in school leadership and is in need of further development—both conceptually and practically. This can be seen manifested in districts with confusion between the role of a mentor and that of a coach, as well as different definitions and uses of coaches (instructional, leadership, teacher) within the same organization. Does your organization have a singular definition for each of these roles, with a picture of how each role complements the other and the differences between the two? In order to identify the best approach for your Leadership Development System (or to use both), it is important to understand the differences between these two approaches to professional development.

While there are similarities between mentoring and coaching, there are also clear differences. Coaching requires specific skills to target identified areas of leadership competencies, while mentoring is more of an overarching umbrella approach to socialization. Davis et al. (2005) have couched coaching within mentoring, articulating it as a specific approach to working with aspiring leaders in administrative training programs. Roberts' (2000) phenomenological study supports this positioning of coaching within the wider frame of mentoring (although Roberts found a unifying definition in the mentoring literature to be elusive). The dichotomy between the two becomes apparent when you peel back the surface layers. One can see how mentoring and coaching can both be used in school districts with school leaders. If mentoring and coaching programs are carefully designed and implemented, the two can complement one another and provide a good support structure for leaders. "Mentoring and coaching processes can serve to augment the succession planning and professional development of districts" (Hopkins-Thompson, 2000, p. 29).

Mentoring

Mentoring is more informal than coaching and relies on professionals working currently in the field, often holding the same job title as the mentee or just one "level higher." Mentors are often "tapped" from the school district the mentee is working in or the same district the aspiring leader is serving in as an intern. Mentors provide insight, socialization, and informal guidance in the routines, processes, and expectations of the school district. Daresh (2004), for example, has defined a mentor as a teacher, guide, counselor, positive role model, and a wise and experienced supervisor.

Mentors also serve as critical friend and as listeners (Duncan & Stock, 2010). A review of the literature reveals "mentoring" has been the predominant mode of providing support to school leaders, but is often done in an informal manner. The Southern Regional Education Board (SREB) and other organizations (such as the Wallace Foundation) have called for more attention to be paid to mentoring aspiring school leaders. It is an important component in the induction process for aspiring and current school leaders and aids in the socialization process for new and aspiring principals (Browne-Ferrigno & Muth, 2006; Daresh, 2004). Mentoring is a process that focuses on the growth of the individual and helps to bridge gaps between theory learned in leadership preparation programs and the reality of practice in the field (Duncan & Stock, 2010). The reality of mentoring in the field is a means to provide socialization and connections and to develop collegial relationships with others in the school district (Browne-Ferrigno & Muth, 2006).

"Although there is widespread acceptance of mentoring as a professional development tool, it has become clear that problems have also accompanied this practice across the United States" (Daresh, 2004, p. 496). While approached as a "panacea" for addressing support deficits in education (Daresh, 2004), mentoring has numerous drawbacks if used exclusively to support aspiring and current school leaders. Mentoring is often seen as a one-way relationship (Daresh, 2004) and paternalistic in nature. This sets up an almost unfair dynamic between the mentor and mentee, especially if the mentee is being mentored by her or his supervisor. Working in the same district as your mentor poses challenges for confidentiality (Bloom et al., 2003).

While not always the practice, mentors can be, and often are, supervisors of the people being mentored. Mentors can also be peers of the mentee, again setting up an unbalanced dynamic. In some cases the mentee can become so dependent on the mentor that a "dependent relationship is formed" (Daresh, 2004). According to Riley (2009, p. 233), "the successful mentoring of new school leaders by their experienced colleagues involves two busy professionals seeking time to conduct enough mentoring conferences to facilitate protégé growth." Therefore, one of the major drawbacks to an overreliance on the use of mentors is that there is a severe time limitation on the parties involved.

Another concern about the concept of mentoring is that it is one word used to define a number of relationships (Daresh, 2004). For example, teachers may be mentored when they enter the profession. Aspiring school leaders in preparation programs are often assigned mentors when participating in their internship activities. Principals can be assigned peer mentors when they begin a new job. The use of one word as an umbrella term does not provide clarity as to the unique requirements of each mentoring relationship (Daresh, 2004).

Several common features emerge from the review of the literature on mentoring:

1. often informal and little training involved for the mentors;
2. initiated most often by the mentee, including identification of the mentor;
3. the mentee is often passive;
4. the focus of the mentoring activities is primarily on socialization and developing collegial relationships;
5. the mentor is typically a colleague in the district at the same job level or one level higher;
6. time limitation is a drawback when the mentor is a current administrator.

Coaching

Coaches are commonplace throughout our lives and, as such, we often take the role and what it entails for granted. There is some history of formal coaching in business (e.g., job and executive coaches), in personal lives (e.g., life coaches), and obviously in athletics. As a profession, coaching leaders in education is an emerging field (Salter, 2008). To operationalize the term, a coach is someone who provides support, motivation, and assistance in achieving goals (either personal or professional).

> Good coaching gets results—and it gets them fairly quickly.
> (Fullan & Knight, 2011, p. 50)

Coaching has gained traction as a popular leadership support mechanism in schools within the past several years. However, the field of school leadership coaching is still new and while there are resources about coaching in sports and business, these are still being formed in the field of education. Nonetheless, educational organizations are beginning to use coaching with school personnel as a strategy to clarify job expectations, match individual and organizational goals, and monitor progress in professional development, primarily in more seasoned staff (Fullan & Knight, 2011).

The word *coaching* derives from the Hungarian word *kocsi* and means "transporting to a desired destination in a comfortable carriage" (Tschannen-Moran & Tschannen-Moran, 2010, p. 7). Coaching principles adhere to adult learning theories, popularized by Malcolm Knowles' theory of andragogy. Definitions of coaching emphasize various aspects of the coaching process and purpose, but often to varying degrees. Duncan and Stock's (2010) definition of coaching reflects Knowles' principles: "Coaching . . . is an action-oriented initiative that impels personal and team learning toward solving problems, with a focus on building organizational capacity . . . Coaches work with people to help them achieve high levels of performance" (p. 297). Lovely's (2004) definition relies on the comparison of mentors and coaches yet does not distinguish clearly between the two. For example, he argues that mentors, more than coaches, are like master principals. Coaches, on the other hand, "go beyond the search for a quick fix by helping beginners see the difference between their intentions and actions. This is done through listening, observation, and inquiry . . ." (p. 62). Leadership coaches, rather than mentors, by virtue of their situation within the school and district context are able to provide a more formalized induction, which research indicates new principals need (Lochmiller & Silver, 2010).

Admittedly, one of the limitations currently around school leadership coaching is the lack of a single definition. Bloom, Castagna, Moir, and Warren (2005) have stated that "coaching is all the rage, yet it enjoys no common definition, and little research has been done on its efficacy" (p. 3). This "complex art," as Tschannen-Moran and Tschannen-Moran (2010) have called coaching in their *Evocative coaching* text, does have a number of definitions, although they are not competing definitions; rather, they share commonalities. Most of the coaching literature that revolves around aspiring and current school leaders refers to this type of coaching as *leadership coaching*. "Leadership coaching is one approach to providing support to leaders by offering opportunities to have a dialogue, seek advice, rehearse, and question key institutional leadership decisions and actions" (Sharratt & Fullan, 2009, p. 49).

Provided below are additional definitions from authors who are doing research on coaching or have published school leadership coaching texts to help guide this approach to educational leadership support.

1. The Evocative Coaching model defines coaching as "calling forth motivation and movement in people, through conversation and a way of being, so they achieve desired outcomes and enhance their quality of life" (Tschannen-Moran & Tschannen-Moran, 2010, p. 7).
2. Robertson (2005, p. 24) asserts that "coaching . . . is a special, sometimes reciprocal, relationship between (at least) two people who work together to set professional goals *and* achieve them."
3. Lovely (2004, p. 63) states "a coach brings about personal transformation by
    - examining how the principal conducts herself and treats others,
    - determining whether the principal capitalizes on opportunities or shies away from them, identifying if the principal sees the difference between systemic and superficial causes of problems,
    - recognizing the principal's ability to remain optimistic even in the face of adversity, and
    - assessing the principal's level of emotional awareness."
4. Bloom et al. (2005) define coaching in a way that describes the relationship between the coach and the coachee. Rather than give a blanket

definition, the authors highlight key andragogy components and then describe the "key elements" of effective leadership coaching: the coach constructs a relationship based upon trust and permission; the coach serves as a different observer of the coachee and the context; the coach and coachee recognize that problems and needs are valued learning opportunities; the coach must be prepared to apply a variety of coaching skills as appropriate to the context and needs of the coachee; the coach is fully present for and committed to the coachee; the coach provides emotional support to the coachee; the coach maintains a fundamental commitment to organizational goals as agreed to by the coachee, and appropriately pushes the coachee to attain them; and the coach practices in an ethical manner.

What these definitions hint at but do not always explicitly state is that coaching is more than "showing the ropes"; it is goal and performance oriented. Contrasted with the mentor's focus on inducting new colleagues into the workplace, or assisting a seasoned but underperforming staff member, coaching tends to address the needs of the new or established professional as those needs relate to organizational goals and performance.

The coaching process involves a high degree of active listening, non-evaluative and non-judgmental questioning, and a collaborative problem-solving practice focused on eliciting the solution from the coachee (as opposed to telling the coachee what to do, which is often typical in mentoring relationships). It assumes a level of expertise of the person being coached, in short. Coaches are formally assigned (by the preparation program or district or other partner provider), unlike the often informal mentors who can frequently be self-selected by the mentee. Leadership coaching is focused on specific job tasks and skills, as opposed to mentoring, where a senior staff member works with a colleague to help promote acculturation and career development. Coaches help break down skills for jobs and provide feedback to the coachee (see Figure 7.1).

Coaches can be used for both current school leaders and aspiring school leaders. While the context is different, the approach is the same. When applied to the aspirant, the aspiring school leader benefits from the aid of a skilled professional who can help guide them in their practicum and internship experiences (Browne-Ferrigno & Muth, 2006). Again,

Leadership Coaching		
coaches receive focused, in-depth, and ongoing training		
Action-Oriented	**Relationships**	**Process-Focused**
- Problem solving - Contextually relevant	- Positive and trusting - Focused on the mentee	- Active listening and observing - Coaches use a variety of skills and strategies - Non-evaluative and non-judgmental - Deliberate and intentional

Figure 7.1 Coaching Features
Source: Author

what differentiates coaching from mentoring is the focus on developing the individual in ways that address organizational improvement goals. Professional development for practicing school leaders needs to be relevant to the lives of assistant principals and principals. Coaching can aid in providing this for principals (Rodriguez-Camps, Rincones-Gomez, & Shen, 2005).

Overall, the literature on leadership coaching reveals several common features: action-oriented and a problem-solving focus; active listening and active dialogue, observing, and asking questions by coaches; there is a positive and trusting relationship; use of multiple skills and strategies in the coaching process by the coach; coaches are provided with focused, in-depth, and ongoing training; contextually relevant; deliberate and intentional; focused on the mentee and often initiated by the coach; and non-evaluative and non-judgmental.

The coaching literature also reveals a strong instructional focus in the coaching conversations. While managerial tasks may be a component of the coaching process, and are admittedly on the minds of most new administrators as they navigate the waters of the principalship, the focus in the literature quickly turns to instructionally centered conversations.

Example from the Field

The Evolution of Leadership Coaching in a District

Leadership Coaching in Hampton City Schools

History

Hampton City Schools (Hampton, Virginia) saw the opportunity to support building principals through coaching and added a Leadership Coach in 2010, writing the position into the Title I grant. "In providing job-embedded training for building administrators, the Title I Leadership Coach will serve as a confidant for principals. The coach will work with building administrators to help identify areas for improvement in schools, serve on School Improvement Teams, discuss goals, and identify strategies to increase student achievement" (HCS Title I Application 2010–11).

Initially, two leadership coaches were hired and spent much of their time researching and developing a framework for coaching leaders within the division. Unfortunately, due to decreases in funding, one position was cut, leaving only one Leadership Coach for the division working with Title I building administrators. Over the past five years, Eric Stone has received extensive coach training and developed a Leadership Coaching Framework that continues to evolve as the needs of the schools and division change. For example, when leadership coaching began in Hampton City Schools, the coaching support service delivery model was based on the Response to Intervention Pyramid where the most challenging schools received the most coaching support in terms of both type and time (see Figure 7.2). Schools with the lowest test scores and most challenging population (due to high poverty, discipline problems, low parent involvement, high teacher turnover, etc.) received more support in terms of time allotment, but principals weren't necessarily buying into the notion of coaching. In other words, it felt like "one more thing" principals were required to do because their schools were in Priority or Focus status, and under the watchful eye of either the state department or the division.

The inverted support model was dropped in favor of a more focused yet flexible model, paired with professional learning opportunities for

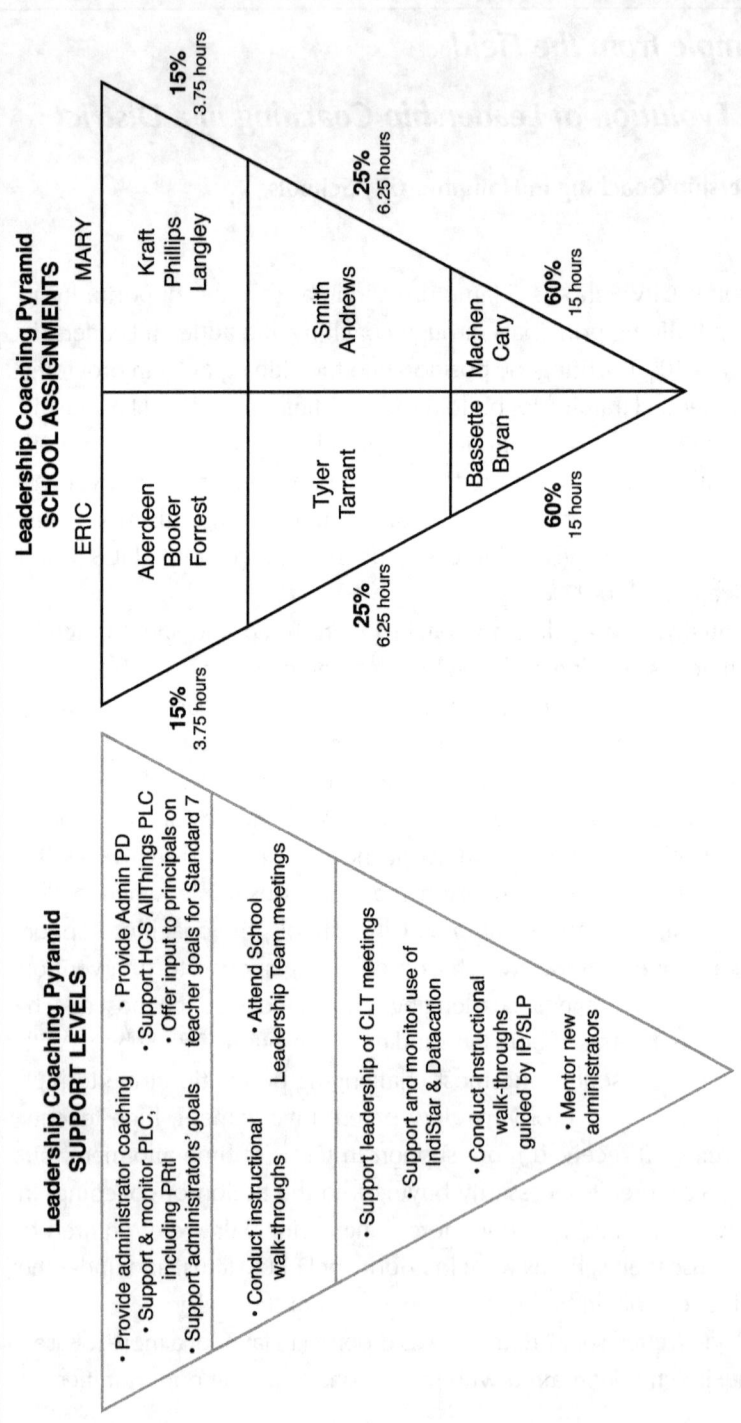

Figure 7.2 Leadership Coaching Pyramid: Support Levels and School Assignments

Source: © Eric Stone. Used with permission.

administrators focused on understanding the "why" behind coaching and how coaching teachers would bring about desired improvement in teaching performance, and thus improved test scores. This worked extremely well, especially since the school division had restructured the Title I service delivery model, creating instructional coaches in the areas of language, arts, and mathematics whose primary role was coaching classroom teachers. Principals were observing instructional coaches and classroom teachers working together and witnessing positive changes in teaching and learning. Coaching was starting to be valued and the whole school division began moving toward a "coaching culture." Last year, the Center for School Transformation staff provided training monthly to principals on the components of Evocative Coaching, which included a conversation model to follow when conducting pre-and post-observation conferences.

Some mindset shifts that occurred which supported this evolution of leadership coaching in Hampton City Schools are shown here:

Mindset Shifts

Leadership Practices	From	To
Pre- and Post-observation conference	Starting with a Supervision Mindset, giving advice, telling the teacher what to do instructionally	Starting with a Coaching Mindset, being an equal partner and collaborator, using effective listening and questioning strategies
Supervision	Supervising teachers equally	Knowing *which* teachers require supervision, mentoring, or coaching AND knowing when to "flex" between practices and differentiate
Evaluation	Evaluating teacher performance based on a list of skills or attributes	Evaluating teacher performance based on goal setting and progress toward goal.
Role of a principal	Expert evaluator	Collaborative coach

Mentoring and Coaching

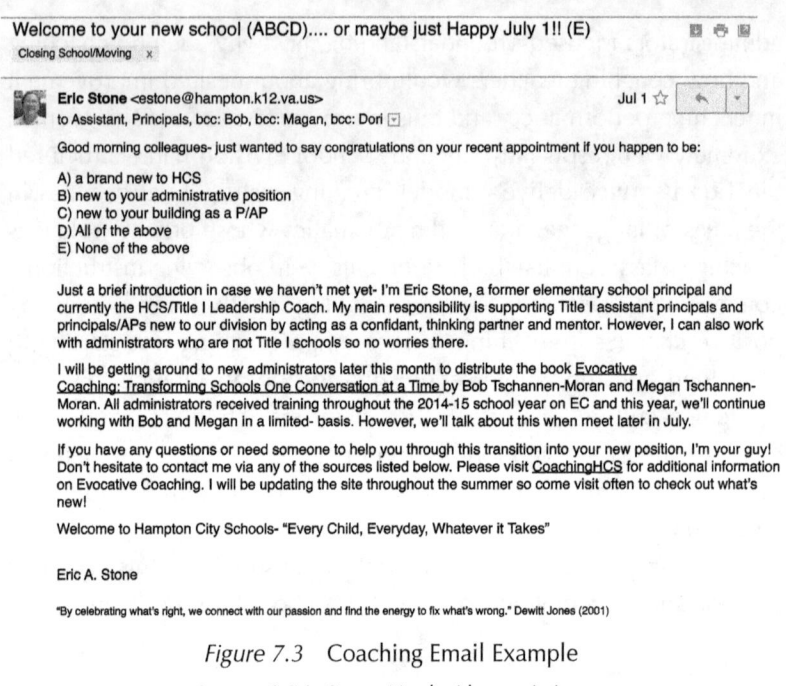

Figure 7.3 Coaching Email Example

Source: © Eric Stone. Used with permission.

Present

Leadership coaching in HCS has been transformed since its inception five years ago. When a new principal or assistant principal is hired, a welcome email is sent out from the Leadership Coach (see the example in Figure 7.3).

The HCS Organizational Learning and Effectiveness Department provides opportunities for supporting new principals throughout the year, beginning with a New Administrator Orientation early in the summer. Key departments within the organization begin forming relationships with administrators while providing snapshots of procedures and small pieces of the organizational puzzle, being careful not to overwhelm the newly hired while alleviating any concerns and stress. The Organizational Learning and Effectiveness Department also provides monthly professional development to all building administrators that is related to HCS Strategic Goals and typically around a theme, such as effective leadership and instructional strategies to implement when working with families living in poverty.

New Administrator Orientation
Monday, July 13, 2015
5th Floor Conference Room
1 Franklin Street
Hampton, VA 23669

8:00am	Welcome and Introductions
8:15am	Public Relations
9:00am	Finance (Kronos, Payroll, Fund 50 & General Accounts)
9:30am	Student Services
10:30am	Information Literacy (*Please bring your charged laptops for this session*)
11:30am	Special Education & 504s
12:00pm	Lunch with Mentors in the 2nd Floor Professional Learning Training Center
1:00pm	Professional Learning Procedures
1:30pm	Human Resources
2:00pm	Closing

Figure 7.4 Administrator Orientation Agenda Example
Source: © Eric Stone. Used with permission.

A sample agenda for the summer New Administrator Orientation is shown in Figure 7.4.

The HCS Administrator Launchpad is also introduced during this orientation. All pertinent information regarding division initiatives, including meeting agendas, meeting files database, meeting feedback, school learning plans, and a designated New Administrators section, is located within this information warehouse, created as a Google site with web access. There are also links to other HCS sites (New Teacher Info, Curriculum Launchpad, Great Lesson Library, and HCS Podcast Library, to name just a few). These resources are available and updated throughout the year and serve as a "one-stop" shop for administrators to access information anywhere, anytime in an efficient manner.

New administrators are also paired with current building principals who serve similar student populations, school enrollments, etc. Central Office administration has the expectation that the pairs meet regularly on a collaboratively set schedule. In this case, HCS principals take on the role of a mentor, providing support to new principals through face to face conversations, phone calls, emails, and sharing ideas and documents that have been effective, e.g., "Welcome Back to School Parent Letters."

The Leadership Coach meets with new administrators (Title I principals and assistant principals) every two weeks. These conversations take on a mentoring or coaching format, depending on the needs of the administrator. Besides individual conversations, the Leadership Coach is also available to meet with the principal and assistant principal as a Collaborative Learning Team (CLT) where all are equal participants and may use this as an opportunity to try out an impending "difficult conversation" with a struggling teacher or challenging parent or colleague. Discussing classroom walk-throughs or observations is more powerful when carried out in a trusting environment, and stronger feedback can be provided to the teacher when constructed by the CLT.

Here Eric Alan Stone shares his experiences of leadership coaching. He currently works in Hampton City Schools as the Title I Leadership Coach, assisting principals and school leadership teams to become more effective in their roles. More coaching strategies from Eric Stone are shared in Chapter 9.

Leadership mentoring and coaching provide critical support for current and aspiring school leaders. Often there is confusion over the differences between coaching and mentoring and therefore organizations crafting a cohesive Leadership Development System should clearly define the roles, responsibilities, and processes involved for each mentor and coach. Ultimately, regardless of the chosen model and view of these two roles, the final approach must be specifically designed for the organization itself in order for it to be a viable and successful model.

Additional Features of a Leadership Development System

A primary goal of this book is to provide Leadership Development System designers in districts and other educational organizations with ways of conceptualizing their own system. While it is not possible to share all of the invaluable practices in place related to educational leadership development, it is possible to share with you a variety of system features and approaches to leadership development that can be incorporated into your work. This chapter contains a few additional program features that can be substantive components of a cohesive Leadership Development System. These were highlighted previously in Chapter 3 and are expanded upon within this chapter. Illustrative examples are also provided to better elucidate how these features can present themselves in a variety of settings.

Cohorts

Cohorts in leadership support initiatives are groups of individuals who go through the same development activities. Often cohorts are grouped according to roles. For example, many leadership preparation programs throughout the US use cohorts with their aspiring leadership students, new principals will connect over an academic year through structured group training activities, or instructional coaches meet in small cohort groups to discuss content specific coaching strategies. Groups of students will engage in a sequence of courses and activities to prepare them for the leadership position. Cohorts work best when adult learning strategies are employed, and are "a part of a socially cohesive activity structure that emphasizes shared authority for learning, opportunities for collaboration, and teamwork in practice-oriented situations" (Davis et al., 2005, p. 10). The development of cohorts should be intentional, with ground rules and cohort norms identified through a facilitated process at the start of the cohort.

In a commissioned study by the Wallace Foundation, Davis, Darling-Hammond, LaPointe, and Meyerson (2005) identified key features of successful leadership development programs. In their review of salient research, they highlighted that cohorts aid in the development of both group and individual knowledge, and that cohorts helped to promote improved learning by cohort members, and contribute to an increased rate of program completion. Using research from Barnett, Basom, Yerkes, and Norris (2000) and Browne-Ferrigno and Muth (2006) to support their work, Davis, Darling-Hammond, LaPointe, and Meyerson (2005) also note that cohorts contribute to persistence in the program, promote creativity in cohort members, and enable cohort members to examine and explore problems through multiple lenses and approaches.

While cohorts are often seen as a strategy for aspiring leadership preparation programs, the use of cohorts with current leaders is a powerful learning tool. Role-alike learning groups can collaborate in an ongoing manner to promote deep learning, as well as to develop support networks for on-the-job challenges. Below is an example of how one district uses cohorts to support role-alike learning of current elementary school leaders.

Example from the Field

Using Cohorts for Current Leadership Development

One thing I would like to highlight is the power of small groups. One initiative I brought to the Newport News Public Schools system is the cohort development model for school leaders. In a large school division/district it is often difficult to meet the development needs of all school leaders. The cohort development approach involved separating the large group of elementary principals into cohorts based on years of experience. Groups were divided into 1–3 years of experience, 4–6 years of experience, 8–10 years of experience

Additional Features of a Leadership Development System

and 10+ years of experience. The cohorts were then involved in one monthly development session held at a host school and one monthly development as a large group. This allowed all elementary school leaders to receive differentiated development based on their level of experience to assist them with implementing division/district initiatives.

Catina Bullard-Clark, Executive Director Elementary Leadership, Newport News Public Schools, Virginia

Cohorts can be used throughout the Leadership Development System. Below, two Principal Coaches from Tulsa Public Schools share how cohorts are used at every stage in the Tulsa Public Schools leadership development pipeline.

Example from the Field

Use of Cohorts in a Leadership Pipeline Initiative

Below are descriptions of pipeline cohorts that Tulsa Public Schools (TPS) uses as a part of a leadership pipeline created to provide high-quality professional development to cohorts.

Emerging Leaders

Teacher leaders' introduction to TPS leadership levers and an exploration of district-based roles for improving teaching and learning (mentoring, coaching, etc.) and school leadership readiness

Levers: Supervision and feedback

Foci: Crucial conversations, Strengthsfinder, introduction to coaching, calibration, six step feedback and McREL

Components: Monthly two hour cohort trainings October to May; job-shadow experience

Assistant Principal Leadership Experience (APLE 1)

First year assistant principal induction

Additional Features of a Leadership Development System

Levers: Supervision and feedback

Foci: CSI observation frame, six steps of feedback, calibration training

Components: Monthly full-day cohort professional development, action research project, monthly job-embedded coaching with assigned principal coach, virtual calibration with TNTP (twice a year)

Assistant Principal Leadership Experience (APLE 2)

Second year assistant principal induction

Levers: Supervision and feedback, data-driven instruction, culture

Foci: Action steps for improving instruction aligned to content, engagement and rigor, development of a team of teachers, leadership of school improvement planning

Components: Monthly half-day site-based cohort professional development, action research project, monthly job-embedded coaching with assigned principal coach, virtual calibration with TNTP (twice a year)

Assistant Principal Leadership Experience Plus (APLE+)

Ongoing professional development for assistant principals with three or more years' experience focused on TPS leadership levers

Levers: Professional learning, curriculum and instructional planning, supervision and feedback, data-driven instruction, culture

Foci: Building walk-throughs and observations, effective feedback, action research planning, site improvement planning, building effective leadership teams, and networking with key stakeholders

Components: Fall and spring series, three two-hour sessions per series; participant choice for course enrollment (one of three)

New Principals Academy (NPA)

Principal induction for first year principals in Tulsa Public Schools

Lever: Culture

Foci: Entry planning, staff and student culture, distributed leadership and teams, coaching APs and teacher leaders, networking with consultancy protocols and onboarding, personal organization and time management

Components: Summer entry planning and onboarding, half-day cohort trainings in fall and spring, job-embedded coaching (twice a month) with principal mentor

Principal Development Leadership Academy (PDLA 2)

Second year principal induction cohort

Levers: Data-driven instruction, curriculum and instructional planning

Foci: Leading team meetings using a DDI cycle focused on standards, student work, lesson planning and assessments aligned to literacy practice to increase student achievement

Components: Monthly half-day site-based cohort study teams differentiated by level with a focus on literacy

Learning Leaders (LL)

High-performing principals exploring and developing their interest, knowledge and skills in leading schools at scale through the ILD role

Levers: ILD strategies to develop TPS instructional leadership levers

Foci: Blended coaching, role of the ILD, evolving role of the principal, liaison with central office, ILD interview tasks

Components: Monthly full-day training (Fri./Sat.), field experiences, peer coaching, and program leader coaching

RELAY Graduate School of Education

Selected cohort of principals, assistant principals, and ILDs committed to the intensive study of the instructional leadership levers and intentional integration into school-based leadership practice

Levers: Culture, data-driven instruction, curriculum and instructional planning, supervision and feedback, professional learning

Foci: Leverage Leadership levers, Teach Like a Champion strategies, Practice Perfect, Driven-by-Data practices

Components: Two week summer off-site intensive training, quarterly off-site training, site-based program leader coaching, documentation of implementation efforts with formal feedback through electronic platform and video practice

> **ILD (Instructional Leadership Director) Coaching and Supervision**
>
> One-on-one job-embedded coaching and supervision support to each principal (at least twice a month) focused on the McREL responsibilities, second order change goals, key district priorities, leadership levers, and school improvement and management needs
>
> **Principal Portfolio Meetings**
>
> Monthly differentiated small group professional development to principals aligned to the leadership levers and key priorities; portfolio meetings provide the opportunity to connect LDD learning to school-based practice
>
> - six hour sessions: August, October, November, December, February, March, April, May (second week of the month)
> - two hour sessions: September, January, and June following the LDD meeting
>
> **Leadership Development Days (LDD)**
>
> Centralized, focused professional development training aligned to the key priorities for all school building leaders
>
> - For principals and APs: seven days
>
> This example from the field was shared by Sheila Armstrong and Debi Boyles, Principal Coaches in TPS. They work together to help develop high-quality school leaders in TPS.

Field-Based Experiences

Field-based experiences, practicums, and internships are all ways that aspiring and current school leaders can experience on-the-job training opportunities. Whether in an aspiring leadership program or in a post-credential development initiative for school leaders, field-based experiences are important for educators to develop skills and abilities for their leadership roles. Well-structured and intentionally designed field-based experiences with guidance and support by trained mentors or coaches fall within the conceptual model of Communities of Practice and legitimate peripheral participation advocated for in this book. Rather than merely telling an aspiring or current school leader to "find experiences" outside of their own work location, well-crafted field-based experiences that are guided by an educational mentor or other leadership expert enable stronger and deeper learning experiences. This "offers a conceptual model with the potential to create well-designed internships that prepare school leaders effectively for their complex roles" (Williams, Matthews, & Baugh, 2004, p. 54).

Generally aspiring leadership programs require some form of internship or other field-based practicum experience. "Sometimes called supervised clinical practice or social practice (Wenger, 1998), situated learning is a well accepted component of professional practice" (Browne-Ferrigno & Muth, 2008, p. 4). The concept behind field-based learning experiences is to provide structured and supervised learning opportunities that give aspiring leaders "educational orientations, perspectives, concepts, language, and behaviors" to change (Browne-Ferrigno, 2007, p. 4) and connect the theoretical constructs learned in the classroom setting to practical settings in PK-12. One of the challenges with many internships is that experiences are held after school hours (Browne-Ferrigno, 2007), during non-instructional times, or during times that do not simulate the same environments and situations as the regular school day (i.e., summer school).

Designers of Leadership Development Systems are strongly encouraged to find ways to allow aspiring and emerging leaders to engage in full-time internship experiences. The ideal experience would be a full year internship in an administrative capacity. Extended internships, those involving full-time work in some capacity throughout an academic year, have been highlighted in several studies on innovative leadership preparation (Bellamy, Crockett, & Nordengren, 2014). For example, the NetLEAD program with Winthrop University, South Carolina, and a consortium of school districts in South Carolina employs a guided year-long internship that allows candidates to have hands-on experiences as a leader. The internship involves the development of principal work samples and allows for site visits to other schools and shadowing administrators.

Another example of an innovative year-long internship is the Northeast Leadership Academy in North Carolina. Through USDE School Leadership Funding, the administrative candidates are released from their teaching

Additional Features of a Leadership Development System

responsibilities for one year. During this internship period interns take on various leadership responsibilities and tackle a problem of practice activity that was identified after completing a school data analysis. In addition to their school leader internship responsibilities, the intern also engages in a full-time summer community internship. In this way the administrators in training are able to connect fully with the school community and contribute to their stakeholders through activities such as grant writing.

Most school districts do not have the funding to support a full year administrative internship for many of those involved in aspiring leadership preparation programs. Additionally, there is frequently a lack of collaboration across institutions to support high-quality internships. Often, communication is lacking between preparation programs and districts, causing less-than-ideal conditions for the administrative internship. A well structured Leadership Development System that incorporates the tenets of successful partnerships and employs sound communication strategies can avoid some of the obstacles to successful internship experiences. Innovative approaches to internship experiences that occur during the school day should be identified by the Leadership Development System designers and the partners of the organization. If aspiring leaders are only provided internship opportunities in an after-school or summer school setting, they will not be adequately prepared to serve as an assistant principal, for example, when they begin their jobs.

The following are eight characteristics of high-quality pre-service principal internships identified by the Southern Regional Education Board (2005, p. 6):

- collaboration between the university and school districts that anchors internship activities in the real-world problems principals face, provides for appropriate structure and support of learning experiences, and ensures quality guidance and supervision;
- an explicit set of school-based assignments designed to provide opportunities for the application of knowledge, skills, and ways of thinking that are required to effectively perform the core responsibilities of a school leader, as identified in state standards and research, and incorporated in the preparation program's design;

- a developmental continuum of practice that progresses from observing to participating in and then to leading school-based activities related to the core responsibilities of school leaders, with analysis, synthesis, and evaluation of real-life problems at each level;
- field placements that provide opportunities to work with diverse students, teachers, parents, and communities;
- handbooks or other guiding materials that clearly define the expectations, processes, and schedule of the internship to participants, faculty supervisors, directing principals, and district personnel;
- ongoing supervision by program faculty who have the expertise and time to provide frequent formative feedback on interns' performance that lets them know how they need to improve;
- directing principals who model the desired leadership behaviors and who know how to guide interns through required activities that bring their performance to established standards; and
- rigorous evaluations of interns' performance of core school leader responsibilities, based on clearly defined performance standards and exit criteria and consistent procedures.

Problem-Based Learning

As discussed in Chapter 4, the use of problem-based learning tools, including case studies and simulations, is very useful to promote adult learning for leadership concepts. In this section, Ken Spero, CEO of Ed Leadership Sims, shares his views on the use of simulations with aspiring and current school leaders. Ken and Ed Leadership Sims' objective is to use computer-based simulation to build resilience, leadership skills, and decision-making capacity in large numbers of education leaders. He has been in the simulation field for more than 25 years, focusing on how to capture and deploy experience in an efficient and scalable manner to enable the adage that "Experience is the Best Teacher." Ken developed the Experience Design Process for simulation development that enables practitioners to articulate their own experiences and the thinking that went into their decisions in a manner which can be effectively shared with others.

Additional Features of a Leadership Development System

Example from the Field

Simulations for Preparing and Developing Leaders

Ed Leadership Sims (ELS) provides experiential leadership development to K-12 administrators using computer-based simulations. ELS' objective is to provide peer-sourced simulations to build resilience, skills, and decision-making capacity in large numbers of educational leaders. The self-paced or team-facilitated simulations are "apprenticeships in a box" to strengthen existing leaders and prepare new ones for the interpersonal challenges they will face in their day to day jobs.

There is a silent crisis undermining School Reform. In any major organizational change effort, especially in a context as complex as the education system, leadership is a key ingredient to success. Of course "leadership" can be defined in many different ways and it is clear that different forms of leadership are required for different situations. However, the ability to communicate, coordinate, and make decisions is key under any circumstance. What makes the Ed Leadership job so challenging is that those abilities are rife with "painful" trade-offs that make them difficult to do under the best of circumstances. The role of leadership in Education is one of the more daunting positions in any industry. Nowhere do we have a group of stakeholders whose demands are more exclusive of each other and that each one can be more irrational than the next. Students, teachers, parents, unions, communities, districts, States, Government, etc., it is practically impossible to satisfy one without dramatically upsetting at least one other. This makes the challenge not just about making good decisions, which is challenging enough, but to be prepared for the negative consequences that are sure to follow from one or more of the stakeholders that view the issue differently.

Simulations for Judgment and Decision Making
From a PD perspective, we can provide leaders with frameworks, insight, strategies and support for this challenge but making decisions in this challenging and evolving context is not something you can easily master because the minefield is constantly shifting and the

consequences manifest clearly in the data below. Experience is really the only way that leaders can get better at making good decisions and good experience is often the result of making mistakes, of failing, and having the wherewithal to learn from it.

How do we provide leaders with the opportunity to fail forward but in a way that is not so painful as to cause burn-out and early exits? This is the role of simulation. By capturing realistic and engaging scenarios that manifest the different inherent challenges and enable leaders to practice Exercising Judgment, to Experience the Consequences of their decisions, and to Get Feedback on what was going on, participants get the opportunity to gain experience where the stakes are low, rather than on the job with potentially devastating negative consequences for a wrong decision.

Simulations as Engaging and Motivating PD
When it comes to professional development of any kind, the first and most important step is Engagement. Much has been written about the challenges of student engagement in K-12. All of the findings apply equally or even more so for the adults/Education Professionals, given the increasing and varied demands on our time. If a participant is not engaged, it does not matter how good the content is or how great an exercise is, it will fail. Therefore, we need to figure out a method for engagement as well as development. In fact, if we could determine a method of engaging participants that further motivates development, wouldn't that be great?

Simulations
We know that people learn in many different ways. This is exacerbated by age differences as well as cultural and geographical. However, the one thing that is shared by all ages and all cultures is a love of stories. There is much research in neuroscience with respect to how we interact with stories but it is clear from both research, anecdotal evidence, and our own experiences that we engage with story-driven interactions more actively, with fewer barriers to learning. This is why simulations are such a powerful modality for professional development. Scenario-based simulations harness the power of storytelling to provide engaging and experiential learning opportunities. The more

compelling the story, the more engaged the viewer/participant gets in the activity and has the opportunity to live vicariously through the characters in the narrative or to experience the topics being addressed. It is no longer about instruction, but rather about experience. And we all know that Experience is the Best Teacher.

Branching scenario simulations capture realistic narratives, based on the real life experiences of practitioner authors, manifest as a form of "choose your own adventure" exercise. In the simulations, leaders are placed into a series of scenarios in which they are challenged with increasingly complicated decisions they must make. They then experience the consequences of their choices as the simulation follows that "branch." The scenarios are, in essence, mini experiences whose impact is influenced by the depth and applicability of the exercise. For our purposes, simulation can be defined as a complex weave of scenarios that are put together to capture a period of time in the life of a character and incorporates content (leadership, ethics, sales, etc.) with context (environment, people, task, etc.) so that it imitates life. This combination of content and context, when placed within the flow of time, enables a participant to experience an issue as it could play out in real life.

Simulations Demonstrate Tradeoffs and Build Resilience
What is it that keeps people from making good decisions? For that matter, what is a "good" decision? This is a growing challenge, especially in the evolving world of Education and Ed Leadership specifically. Because of the combination of increased accountability at lower levels in Districts and Schools and of the increased breadth and diversity of the stakeholders, the consequences of even seemingly low-level decisions have much greater reach. This is further exacerbated by the ready access to overwhelming amounts of information, both inside the School and also for parents/communities. This data stream is filled with both meaningful and meaningless data, but being able to determine which is which helps to increase the risk of analysis paralysis and is intimidating to even the most seasoned leaders and decision makers. From a Leadership Development perspective, how can we address this challenge in a compelling and scalable manner?

Simulations are very powerful because they provide an opportunity for us to contextualize the learning for our leaders or those aspiring to lead. When the targeted learning objectives require some kind of change (either behavioral or skill development) in the leaders, teaching is often not enough and experience is required. Simulation provides an opportunity for leaders and leadership teams to have to think critically and exercise judgment in realistic scenarios, to create muscle memory around thinking and not being mindless. It then provides an opportunity for the leaders to experience consequences so that they can expand their experience portfolios with meaningful experiences that they can draw upon in real life. Lastly, the simulation experience provides insight into the learning through feedback which helps to crystallize what they experienced and to "connect the dots."

When it comes to these context-driven issues, the challenge is not just to make people more comfortable with making decisions but to be comfortable making the tough decisions and solving the tough problems. It is when there is no good answer or when the best answer also has significant negatives associated with it where the real challenge is. That is where we need to create a situation where the focus is not on making our professional development feel "good," because that will not always happen. We want to provide leaders with the practice of making those difficult decisions where they know that even if they make the optimal choice, parts of the outcome will be bad. Simulation provides a context for this kind of meaningful learning-by-doing and this is the role and function of a Trade-off report or Scorecard.

Building Conscious Competence in Leadership
Mindlessness is a key driver of failure in decision making. We often make decisions without critically thinking about the situation we are facing. Humans are creatures of habit. Executing a skill or making a decision without much thought—"Unconscious Competence"—is considered a sign of expertise. But to be mindful, we need to avoid letting habit dictate the way we approach certain situations. By being mindful we can properly maintain our expertise and be able to shift our skills and behaviors as necessary.

The overall goal of scenario-based simulation is not to provide participants with a recipe for effective leadership, but to demonstrate to K-12 Leaders that they need to fully understand the situation they are facing, evaluate it, identify possible responses, and choose the most appropriate solution. In other words, the focus of the simulation is to encourage judgment or *Conscious Competence*.

To do this, the scenarios need to be written to reflect the types of decisions that the leaders face in real life. When participants are faced with a decision in a simulation scenario, there are alternative options to choose from that should provide:

- Valid alternative courses of action. This encourages the leaders to consider different alternatives based on their respective tradeoffs. Choosing between valid courses of action helps to remove the blinders that many K-12 Leaders wear with regard to the habits in their buildings they have developed and the myopic viewpoints they may have on certain issues.
- Opportunities to choose both mindful and mindless courses of action. Leaders get to experience the costs and benefits of Conscious (mindful) versus Unconscious (mindless) thinking through the discussion prompted by the simulation when doing it in groups or through feedback provided in the simulation.

Much has been written on the challenges of mindful decision making and what I have experienced over the years is the many ways that simulations can help to build muscle memory around being Consciously Competent irrespective of the skills being addressed both in their content but also in how they are delivered. It brings to mind the adage "Give a man a fish . . . but Teach a man to fish . . ."; simulation is powerful because of how it can address many of the challenges to mindful decision making.

Three Ways Scenarios Encourage Mindfulness

Simulations also encourage mindful behavior by encouraging information gathering from multiple sources, placing focus on both process and outcomes, and providing shared context for learners.

Gathering Information

Scenarios and simulations can give participants access to sources of information that might assist their decision-making processes. For example, in a simulation on managing change, participants take over the life of a leader in a building or district office. In the story, the other stakeholders in the simulation include the leader's team and/or staff, the Board or District (bosses), teachers, parents, students, etc. At any point in the decision-making process, participants can

- call a meeting with their teams in order to get their feedback on any particular issue,
- walk around the building to access the "grapevine" and get a sense of what is happening, or
- call their respective stakeholders to discuss a problem or simply to touch base.

This simulation allows participants to obtain information that will help them address the problems and decisions facing their simulated companies. The many choices for interaction offered in the simulation remind participants that they may not always know all the answers, but that the information they need to optimize their decision making is usually within arm's reach.

Balancing Outcomes and Processes
Another issue that is both a cause and effect of mindlessness is what is referred to as outcome orientation, which is prevalent in the business world. One of the interesting paradoxes that managers face lies in planning for the long term and managing for the short term with respect to quarterly financial reports to shareholders and the like. This orientation has caused many managers to be totally focused on outcomes without any concern for process "as long as it gets done."

In order to address this lack of consideration for process, scenarios can be designed such that the variables in the skills report are what drive the quantitative results. In fact, in some simulations, participants do not ever see a financial report within the simulation. The idea is for them to understand that in reality it is process that will consistently drive results and improve outcomes.

Providing Common Reference Points
Another benefit that scenarios provide is a shared context for participants. Individuals or groups who face a particular decision

after participating in a simulation enjoy a common reference point or context. This shared context opens the lines of communication between the individuals in the decision-making process, allowing them to form a common understanding of the issue at hand and how it can be resolved.

Simulations for Social Learning and Shared Experience
Playing simulations in teams increases their power for professional development dramatically because of the Social Learning aspect of the deployment and the opportunity for individuals to benefit from the Shared Experience with their peers. The major theme in what makes simulations so powerful as a vehicle for learning and development is that experience is the best teacher. Simulations, designed properly, can approximate experience in key ways that enable participants to learn by doing in contextual issues. They grow from trying "stuff" out and experiencing the consequences of their choices, both good and bad, and having to deal with the outcomes. With simulation, the focus shifts away from Teaching and is more about Application and Resilience as it is not about getting it right. The key issue revolves around gaining experience in a realistic context so that judgment can be improved when the issues are faced in real life.

In thinking about the benefits that simulations offer in support of Experience being the Best Teacher, it is very easy to focus solely on the benefits to the individual student. After all, the simulation offers the student the opportunity to apply and learn from the experience they have with the sim. However, the true efficacy of this approach can be better seen when simulations are played in groups/teams. As human beings we are, at our core, habit forming creatures and have a tendency to seek out the most comfortable way to get things done and stick with it, even when it may not be the best approach. This is part of the benefit of simulation, to provide opportunities for students to gain perspective on the benefits of other approaches. Along these lines, human beings are also social creatures and crave contact with others. Therefore, when simulations are delivered to groups/teams, it provides an opportunity to harness both aspects of being human to provide for a highly engaging and developmental experience. By doing simulations in groups, participants are able to enhance the benefits of this approach through the engagement of Social Learning and the opportunity for Shared Experience. Participants have the opportunity to have their biases challenged, in a non-confrontational way, as they work with their peers to make decisions in a collaborative manner. Having the opportunity to hear others' perspectives on issues and to work toward consensus to make decisions helps to improve judgment in an organic and fun manner and opens up the opportunity for ongoing discussion and collaboration to help establish a more robust learning culture in the district or building.

Simulation Authoring
Simulation is not a science; it is really just a way of organizing one's thinking, and through the Simulation Development or Experience Design Process practitioners (Leaders) can efficiently learn to organize their experiences in a simulation manner that is both beneficial to write and can also be appreciated/enjoyed by others. The objective is not to capture or present "history" but rather to capture the thinking that was happening in the experience, possibly around what was done, but also what was not and why. What could have happened along different pathways, and why? This is where the valuable contextual insights are articulated and captured and can then be deployed for more broad and shared experience. Simulations provide an opportunity to add to our experience portfolio by exercising judgment and experiencing the consequences of our choices in a safe place—"The opportunity to Fail Forward."

To see more about simulations for Leader Development and PD, as well as to get access to try a simulation out, visit the ELS website at: www.edleadershipsims.com. Below are descriptions of a few of the simulations currently in the library and brief descriptions that describe the nature of the scenarios.

Dress Code—As the leader of an elementary school, concerns from staff have been raised regarding the clothing being worn by one of your teachers. In this simulation, you will need to decide how you address those concerns and balance those concerns with other issues that have arisen regarding the same teacher.

Bully—This simulation is based around a collaborative teaching team. There is one teacher on the team, newer to the school but a

Additional Features of a Leadership Development System

mid-career teacher, who is "not a team player." The simulation begins with another teacher on the team coming to the school leader and expressing concern over the way the disruptive teacher is behaving. As the school leader, you participate in a team meeting and witness behavior that is inappropriate and over the top. The simulation goals relate to school culture and climate, conflict management, and responding to teacher concerns.

Angry Parent—A parent at the high school where you are the school leader goes to a school board meeting to complain about the way the girls' basketball coach is treating the players on the team. You must decide how you address the parent's concern and the alleged behavior of the winningest coach in school history.

Academic Goal Setting—This simulation is based around a veteran social studies teacher in a middle school. The teacher has set goals that are not aligned with the new school goals or the Common Core standards. As the school leader, you must decide what steps you will take to try to move this teacher toward alignment with the school goals, and outside his comfort zone.

This example from the field about simulations was shared by Ken Spero, CEO of Ed Leadership Sims.

There are many different program features to consider when developing a cohesive Leadership Development System. Cohorts, grounded in a research-based design, offer an effective structure to develop groups of leaders. The cohort structure allows strong networking to take place, creating connections within the cohort that can have lasting benefits for all members of the group. Field-based experiences also have a profound and long-term impact on the development of leaders. Intentionally crafted experiences provide leaders with valuable hands-on opportunities to connect theoretical constructs of leadership to the practical realities of the job. Other practical opportunities include problem-based activities and simulations that cohorts of leaders and aspiring leaders can engage in to critically understand different leadership situations and approaches to addressing challenges of practice in a low-risk environment.

Adding to Your Leadership Development Toolkit

The leadership development strategies and resources in this chapter are taken directly from practice. These practical, real-life tools are grounded in research and experience. Of course, there are many more activities in use, and by deploying the Open Systems concept of the Leadership Development Ecological Framework the Leadership Development System designers in your organization should cultivate partnerships with other educational institutions to identify more that will work in yours. Ultimately, the designers of the Leadership Development System should work to craft their own strategies that best fit the needs of the system. The activities and processes can be modified from the ones outlined here or be completely different. Familiarity with the variety of strategies and resources available will enable system designers to create processes and activities that maximize internal capacity and help build the skill sets for exemplary leadership.

Aspiring Leader Development Observation Tools

Dr. Tricia Browne-Ferrigno, Professor of Educational Leadership Studies at the University of Kentucky, shares insights into different tools and processes to help prepare aspiring school leaders for field-based instructional observations. Current school leaders in a district Leadership Development System can also use these tools as part of an ongoing leadership development and support system. First, some background is provided on the Principal Preparation Program at the University of Kentucky, followed by an overview of the observation processes. Three tools are then provided for use in your system.

In the Commonwealth of Kentucky, the certificate for school leaders is called Professional Certificate for Instructional Leadership—School Principal, All Grades. Applicants to any pre-service preparation program must meet the following prerequisites:

- Qualify for or hold a Kentucky teaching certificate,
- Completion of at least three years' full-time teaching in P12 setting,
- Successful completion of a master's degree in education with cumulative grade point average of at least 3.0 on a 4.0 scale, and
- Recommendation by a superintendent or other district-level administrator who attests to applicant's educational leadership and professionalism.

The professional reading and learning activities within the program are aligned with the Interstate School Leaders Licensure Consortium (ISLLC) Standards (Council of Chief State School Officers, 2008), the International Society for Technology in Education (ISTE) Standards for Administrators (ISTE, 2009, which replaced the Technology Standards for School Administrators of 2001) and the Dispositions, Dimensions, and Functions for School Leaders adopted by Kentucky as the framework for preparing P12 educational leaders.

The Principal Preparation Program offered by the Department of Educational Leadership Studies (EDL) at the University of Kentucky (UK) was designed to prepare candidates to meet or exceed current and emerging expectations for P12 school principals. Candidates who successfully complete all program requirements are awarded the Specialist in Education (EdS) degree in Educational Leadership Studies by UK and are recommended for Level II principal certification and Rank 1 of the Education Professional Standards Board.

Like all other EDL programs linked to advanced teacher certification, the EDL Principal Preparation Program requires candidates, who typically are working full time as classroom teachers, to complete a variety of field-based, often job-embedded, assignments that enhance transfer of learning to practice. During the first two semesters of the program, candidates conduct five required classroom observations, completed during EDL 706 Leadership in Learning-Centered Schools I and EDL 707 Leadership in Learning-Centered Schools II, that follow the pre-conference–observation–post-conference format. Each interview focuses on a specific aspect of supervision (i.e., observation of learning activities, observation of teaching strategies, observation of assessments in core-content class, observation of assessments in specials or elective class). At least two observations must be conducted in settings that include students who represent diverse student subgroups (e.g., English language learners, special education students, economically disadvantaged students, members of minority groups, students in gifted programs). Candidates are encouraged to conduct at least two observations in grade-level or discipline classrooms different from their current teaching assignment, and if possible in a classroom within a school level different from where they teach. The last prompt on each of the observation report forms asks candidates to reflect on what they learned through completing the assignment.

Contact Professor Tricia Browne-Ferrigno (tricia.ferrigno@uky.edu) for permission to use these forms designed for her classes (111 Dickey Hall, University of Kentucky, Lexington, KY 40506-0017; 859-257-5504; website: http://leadership.uky.edu).

EDL 706, Leadership in Learning-Centered Schools I
Classroom Observation Report

Diverse settings are defined as classrooms

1. In school where candidate works that serves different student sub-populations (e.g., English language learners, special education students, economically disadvantaged students, members of minority groups, students in gifted programs);
2. In school level different from school where candidate works (e.g., elementary, middle, high); or
3. In other learning environments (e.g., early childhood centers, alternative schools, technical schools).

Two classroom observations must be completed while candidate is enrolled in EDL 706 (first semester of program)—one focused on learning, one focused on teaching. Use this form for both observations. The intent of these observations is to expand candidate's awareness of and understanding about how student characteristics (e.g., limited English proficiency, learning disabilities, poverty, ethnicity/race, high potential for learning) and school conditions (e.g., rural versus urban schools, elementary versus secondary schools, high performing versus low performing schools) may impact students' opportunities for learning and their academic achievement.

Adding to Your Leadership Development Toolkit

A form must be completed after each observation and then uploaded to candidate's electronic portfolio. Candidate may use as much space as needed in space immediately below each prompt to respond fully.

Name:			
Date of observation:		Location of observation:	

Describe the classroom observed:
Describe things observed that are unique in classroom:
Summarize topics discussed during debriefing with teacher whose classroom was observed:
Describe lessons you learned about P12 student achievement from conducting this observation:
Reflect about principal's role and responsibilities in conducting classroom observations:

Copyright © Tricia Browne-Ferrigno (2012)

EDL 707, Leadership in Learning-Centered Schools II
Classroom Learning Observation Report

Diverse settings are defined as classrooms
1. In school where candidate works that serves diverse student populations (e.g., English language learners, special education students, economically disadvantaged students, members of minority groups, students in gifted programs);
2. In school level different from school where candidate works (e.g., elementary, middle, high); or

3. In other learning environments (e.g., early childhood centers, alternative schools, technical schools).

One classroom observation focused on student learning must be completed while candidate is enrolled in EDL 707 (second semester of program). The intent of these observations is to expand candidate's awareness of and understanding about how characteristics (e.g., limited English proficiency, learning disabilities, poverty, ethnicity/race, high potential for learning) and school conditions (e.g., rural versus urban schools, elementary versus secondary schools, high performing versus low performing schools) impact P12 students' opportunities for learning and their academic achievement.

A form must be completed after each observation and then uploaded to candidate's electronic portfolio. Candidate may use as much space as needed in space immediately below each prompt to respond fully.

Name:			
Date of observation:		Location of observation:	

Describe the classroom observed:
Describe things observed that are different from your own classroom:
Summarize topics discussed during your debriefing with teacher whose classroom your observed:
Describe the lessons you learned about P12 student achievement from conducting this observation:
Reflect about changes in your professional practice that resulted from conducting this observation:

Copyright © Tricia Browne-Ferrigno (2012)

EDL 707, Leadership in Learning-Centered Schools II
Classroom Assessment Observation Report

Diverse settings are defined as classrooms

1. In classrooms with diverse student subgroups (e.g., English language learners, special education students, economically disadvantaged students, members of minority groups, students in gifted programs), and
2. If possible, at a different-level school from the one where candidates work (e.g., teacher from elementary school conducts observation in a middle school).

Two observations focused on classroom assessments must be completed while candidate is enrolled in EDL 707 (second semester of program). The intent of these observations is to expand candidate's awareness of and understanding about how assessments are utilized to assure students' learning and their academic achievement. A form must be completed after each observation and then uploaded to candidate's electronic portfolio. Candidate may use as much space as needed in space immediately below each prompt to respond fully.

Observer's name:			
Date of observation:		Location of observation:	
Content area or subject observed:		Standard observed and assessed:	

Describe type(s) of assessment implemented:
- What intentional assessments are observed (based on pre-conference with teacher)?
- What unintentional assessments are observed?

Analyze the congruency between the academic standard and the assessment(s):
- Does(do) the assessment(s) truly assess the standard being taught?
- Does(do) the assessment(s) assess the entire standard or just parts?
- Does(do) the assessment(s) assess the correct depth/level of the standard?

Adding to Your Leadership Development Toolkit

Describe how assessment(s) is(are) used during the lesson: • Is assessment used to certify learning? • Is assessment used to support learning? • Is assessment an integral part of learning?
Discuss who used the information generated by the assessment(s) observed: • What evidence exists that the teacher uses the assessment information? • What evidence exists that the students use the assessment information?
Reflect about the type and use of assessment(s) in the classroom:

Copyright © Tricia Browne-Ferrigno (2012)

Aspiring Leader Program Design

Cohesive Leadership Development Systems have various subcomponents that comprise the holistic system. These subcomponents are the heart of the system and each one must be fully articulated. Often, it is helpful to have a graphical representation of the system that accompanies the broader written description. Figure 9.1 depicts a generic framework for an aspiring leaders component. The basic design shown is shared as a starting point for your own system's approach. This can be enhanced, expanded upon, and changed to fit the contextualized needs of the educational organization.

Blogging about Practices

Many districts have incorporated blogging into their Leadership Development System. A lead blogger, or a host of bloggers depending on the size of the district, is responsible for different blogging topics, including assistant principal advice, principal tools and tips, and teacher leader strategies. Dr. Garett Smith, Executive Director for Elementary School Leadership in Newport News, Virginia, shares an example from one of his leadership blog posts.

Adding to Your Leadership Development Toolkit

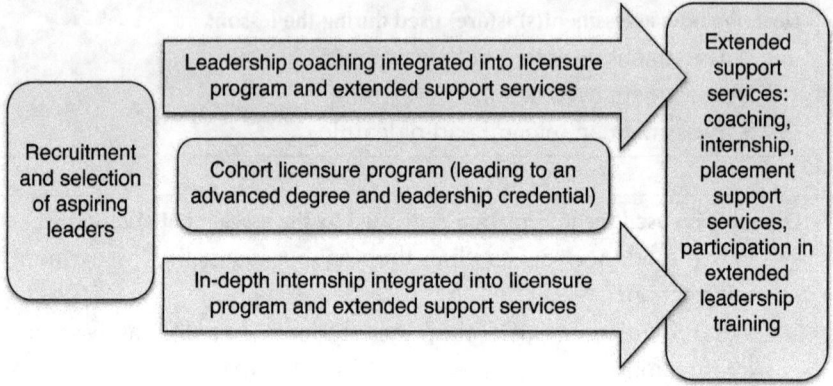

Figure 9.1 Aspiring School Leaders Framework
Source: Author

School Climate and Culture

Practically anyone who has aspired to school administration has received this advice: "Don't make any changes in your first year." This is a prevailing myth in instructional leadership. The reasoning behind this thinking is that a new principal should take a full year to assess the programs and people in place before making any substantial decisions.

A new leader in any organization is presented with a great opportunity to impart his/her vision on that organization. And, fair or not, everyone is watching to see what happens at the start of your tenure. You can say anything you want, but your employees will judge you by your actions. If you want to sit and wait it out your first year, that opportunity will pass you by.

Let's break down what our omniscient advisors mean when they talk about not making any "changes." Most likely they're talking about schedules, duty stations, class/subject/grade level assignments, lunch times, and other details that fall more under the category of management than leadership. Maybe our advisors have a valid point about not changing infrastructure. But managers, unlike leaders, aren't charged with implementing change.

The leader in any organization creates the climate and enhances the culture. I once asked a class of teachers/aspiring principals what they could do, immediately, to make a positive impact on their school's climate.

Adding to Your Leadership Development Toolkit

Among the responses:

- write thank you notes
- give positive, unexpected feedback to both students and teachers
- make positive phone calls home on behalf of students
- notice student achievements or improvements in grades
- take the initiative to participate in volunteer activities such as school beautification projects
- come to work every day with a positive attitude, don't let your bad moods show through to students or teachers
- be seen throughout the school rather than staying in your office
- speak to and get to know all employees
- perform bus duty—be visible to students and parents
- learn everyone's names, students and staff, as soon as possible
- enter the classroom and interact with the students—don't just stick your head in the classroom
- have food at staff meetings
- utilize students to assist with school functions and events—safety patrol, office and teacher assistants, guides for special events and for visitors
- attend extracurricular activities and after school events, intramurals, after school enrichment programs
- coordinate teacher recreational activities that allow teachers to develop relationships outside the classroom and break down barriers between teachers and teams
- institute a wellness program
- teach classes yourself or tutor students.

Even though they had no administrative experience, these teachers possessed a clear understanding of the Principal's role in establishing the school climate. They wondered how a person could forget such basic ideas when they moved from the classroom to the Main Office. They declared that they would remember when they got their opportunity.

Changes to school climate and culture are real and lasting. It all starts at the top. As Whitaker (2003) says, "when the principal sneezes, everyone catches a cold."

Coaching Feedback

Leadership Coach Feedback to Principals and Responses

Eric Stone, Title I Leadership Coach, shares coaching feedback strategies below.

> One strategy that is critical in coaching is providing feedback—the more specific, the better! It is sad how little feedback principals actually get, and when it is given, it is typically not specific, i.e., "you are doing a great job," or not positive. So, I make it a point to provide specific, positive feedback to my principals and School Leadership Team members. Not only am I certain it makes their day, but it energizes them to "pay it forward" to their staff and colleagues.

Examples of Feedback Provided by Leadership Coach (Shared by Eric Stone)

> "What a powerful session this morning. I hope you feel a bit calmer and focused as a result of our time together. After you read my notes, feel free to call me and we can set aside more time to address any one of the items you wish to pursue."

> "Thanks again for the opportunity to support your professional growth as a building leader. Your mindset is so positive—I know that you will transition well along this journey."

> "You did a great job sharing your Academic Review experience with your colleagues yesterday. The 'Reflections on the Academic Review Process' document will be helpful to your colleagues. The AR Benefits section provided specific examples regarding how *your school* has utilized this process to improve such areas as providing feedback and closely examining the current practices in the building against 'best practices' and making needed changes. The actions that were shared in the 'As a result we have . . .' section were all positively stated and focused on growth and improvement. Thanks for your leadership to *your school* and HCS. As always, if there is anything I can do to support your development as a leader, give me a holler! Have a great weekend. E"

> "Today's conversation highlights:
> + The whole writing piece is something you are figuring out—yea!! Writing waiver releases, memos, press releases, etc. will become second nature before you know it!

+ Your knowledge and experience working with *the school* has solidified . . . You stated you were creating the position of Liaison ***** plan from the ground up—this is something you are an expert in and enjoy doing."

"Your comment about the growth of the School Leadership Team this year was spot on! Each member provided in-depth, clear descriptions of the slide information—they knew the content of the slides and only used them for supplemental support. They provided detailed examples of what the students were 'doing and not doing correctly' and identified skills such as fact fluency via domino games, measuring angles, and protractor manipulation issues. What a great story about isosceles and equilateral triangles and the need to use specific vocabulary and tech tools. The entire presentation from start to finish was awesome—it is quite evident that the team is an extension of the Admin and vice versa. Excellent job today!"

Coaching Log

Sheila Armstrong and Debi Boyles, Principal Coaches in the Tulsa Public Schools (TPS) system, share a strategy they have employed to capture the conversations that take place in coaching sessions.

> Principal coaches utilize a Leadership Coaching Tool that was adapted from the New Teacher Center Collaborative Assessment Log. This log is printed on carbon copy paper and allows the coach and coachee to keep a record of the completed coaching log. The focus of the session is pre-determined based on the previous session's "next steps". Coaches pre-plan questions to assist coachees in identifying 1) What's working, 2) Challenges/Concerns, 3) Principal's Next Steps, 4) Coach's Next Steps. The tool also includes a section to progress monitor work toward the McREL Balanced Leadership Framework. Our framework includes Managing Change, Focus of Leadership, and Purposeful Community.

The Collaborative Assessment Log enables coaches to focus on both positive aspects of what is working for the coachee and any problems of practice the coachee is currently facing, in addition to next steps for both the coachee and the coach. Using a tool like this is not only beneficial while in the coaching session, but provides a means of documenting the coaching conversation and identifying tangible next steps for action.

Cohort Branding

Identity in cohorts develops over time, but begins forming from the minute the cohort members are identified. Shaping identity to promote a collaborative mindset and a learning orientation can be helped through a process of cohort branding. Cohort leads (those responsible for organizing and coordinating the cohort) can engage in an innovative approach to help solidify cohort identify. The cohort is split into smaller subgroups. These subgroups should be intentionally designed by the cohort lead to achieve a pre-identified purpose (i.e., mixing content areas, differentiating based upon experience level, etc.). Over the course of a set time period (three months is suggested) the cohort engages in the process of cohort branding.

Each subgroup is charged with developing an emblem that represents the whole group, along with a vision statement to support the group. Over a process of several weeks or months the subgroups present the emblem and vision statement to the whole cohort. Through a consensus-making process, the cohort lead guides group members to identify the emblem and vision statement that best represents the group. The emblem can then become a hallmark visual of their participation in the cohort. The example in Figure 9.2 is shared from the HCS–ODU Leadership Cohort partnership between Hampton City Schools and Old Dominion University in Virginia.

Festival of Ideas

The Festival of Ideas is an innovative professional development strategy that allows *all* participants in a conference setting to share school and/or district best practices. These practices should be anchored in the strategic plan for the district or school or state standards.

Directions: Participants are asked to provide a 10–15 minute presentation describing a best practice from the school or district level in advance of a conference. Schools and districts are partnered with other schools and

Adding to Your Leadership Development Toolkit

Figure 9.2 HCS–ODU Leadership Cohort Partnership Emblem
Source: Author

districts to engage in the Festival of Ideas throughout the course of the professional learning institute (conference). If this is an internal conference or institute (internal to the district), then leaders from different schools and departments should be seated in a way that allows leaders to share their own practice and learn about a variety of innovative practices that will benefit their own work setting. In order to prepare for the Festival of Ideas, participants should be asked to submit a brief write-up about their featured best practices.

Best practices can be submitted online, using an online survey tool such as surveymonkey, or emailed to a coordinator of the event. In this way, the best practices are captured and cataloged in an electronic or print resource to use after the conference. The information you will need on the form for participants to fill out is as follows:

1. Contact information (name, work location information, phone, and email)
2. Strategic plan or standards references
3. Background about school or district
4. Priorities and strategies for improvement

5. Description of your emerging best practice—anchored to the domains *(Describe the practice. Highlight key elements. Discuss how it evolved.)*
6. Indicators of impact and improvement
7. Description of key supports leading to success
8. Summary of key lessons learned

This leadership development tool was provided by Dr. Al Bertani. Dr. Bertani is a Senior Advisor with the Urban Education Institute at the University of Chicago in the United States and Senior Associate with the Innovation Unit in England.

The Festival of Ideas shared by Dr. Bertani has been used for a number of years at the Alaska Staff Development Institute's annual conference of school leaders. Below is an example response provided for the annual conference in Alaska.

Example Response

Background Information about the School

We are a remote village in the Humble school district and we have 174 students K-12. Principal has been in village for 2 years and we have 3 new teachers this year. We use Learning Town for reading and Saxon for math. We have used Aimsweb for 2 years.

Priorities and Strategies for Improvement for 2010–2011

Priorities: Assessment & Curriculum Strategies: 1. Fully implement Aimsweb screening assessment. 2. Provide additional professional development for teachers. 3. Use screening data in teachers meetings. 4. Become efficient at using Aimsweb reports for examining student achievement.

Description of Your Emerging Best Practice—Anchored to the Domains *(Describe the practice. Highlight the key elements. Discuss how it evolved.)*

Fully implement Aimsweb screening assessment.

1. Principal monitors and supports teachers with giving the assessment 3 times a year to all students and entering the data into the database—last year we only assessed some students part of the year.

2. Provide additional professional development for teachers. Teachers will receive formal inservice from CORE in the fall and winter when results are in. We didn't know how to use the reports very efficiently last year and needed lots of practice.

3. Use screening data in teacher meetings—principal participates in teacher meetings to analyze data and make instructional plans. All teachers will bring data to teacher meetings. Reports and data sets will be identified for the meeting and communicated to teachers. We will use criterion referenced data for analysis.

4. Become efficient at using Aimsweb reports for examining student achievement—learning plans will be developed for students who fall below Benchmark on the screening assessment. Principal will use the learning plans to guide principal walk-throughs. Last year we didn't address student needs after looking at the data. We were more concerned with overall performance rather than individual students.

Indicators of Impact and Improvement

Improved results: spring 2008–09 results, 24% of students in first grade were proficient with RCBM, 37% of students in Kindergarten were proficient with PSF, 34% of students in fourth grade were proficient with RCBM; spring 2010 results, 46% of students in first grade were proficient with RCBM, 61% of students in Kindergarten were proficient with PSF, 51% of students in fourth grade were proficient with RCBM.

Description of Key Supports Leading to Success

Teachers now understand the purpose of the assessments and how to use the reports to look at student progress. We are better at knowing when a child is at risk for reading failure. When a student is identified as "at risk," we meet as a group to build a plan for that child for more intervention or targeted instruction. The learning plans help us focus on that child very specifically and watch their progress closely. Teachers are now excited to get results and are beginning to believe that student achievement can increase dramatically.

The principal's involvement was the most influential factor. Having the leader attend the meetings and hold teachers accountable created the expectations and focus that the school needed. Identifying the reports that we use was also helpful as there are so many reports to choose from in the database. Professional development made a huge difference in creating confidence with teachers and analyzing data.

Summary of Key Lessons Learned

1. Principal participation makes a huge difference. 2. Professional development is critical for success. 3. Practice with analysis brings increased confidence. 4. Individual student success creates overall school success. 5. Analyzing the data without changing instruction has little impact. 6. Principal expectations and monitoring those expectations make a huge difference.

Field Projects

Field-based learning is an important part of any Leadership Development System. There are any number of field-based projects an aspiring leader or current leader can engage in during a field project. Below is a description of a two-phase field-based project used in the Building a High Quality Leadership Pipeline for LAUSD's Autonomous Schools project.

Year 1: *Building Strong Leadership Teams and Distributed Leadership Model*—Aspiring leadership candidates analyze the leadership team and the use of distributed leadership at the school site. This analysis involves examining how teachers are involved in multiple leadership opportunities. Findings from the analysis are used to create a plan to enhance distributed leadership in the school and implement the plan. There is also a strong focus on equity and excellence.

Year 2: *Instructional Change Inquiry*—The leadership candidates, in collaboration with the leadership team at the school, design an inquiry question based on a problem of practice to make a demonstrable impact on instruction in the school, including curriculum and assessment. Multiple measures of data are incorporated into the process and must include goals around cultural, structural, or instructional aspects of the school. Program partners create rubrics tailored to the project designed by the candidate to assess the efficacy of the intervention.

Holistic Design Concept Model

Figure 9.3 shows a holistic design concept used by Old Dominion University's Educational Leadership Program in Norfolk, Virginia. This conceptual model has informed the development of leadership cohort partnerships with over 20 school districts over the past decade. While always in a process of continuous improvement, this concept model provides grounds for productive dialogue around values, beliefs, and expectations in a cohort leadership preparation program with district partners. Leadership Development System designers can use this model, or adapt it to fit the organization's needs, for creating a holistic system for leadership preparation and development. The five principles of the model can help guide the crafting of the whole system, as well as reflecting on and designing individual pieces of the system.

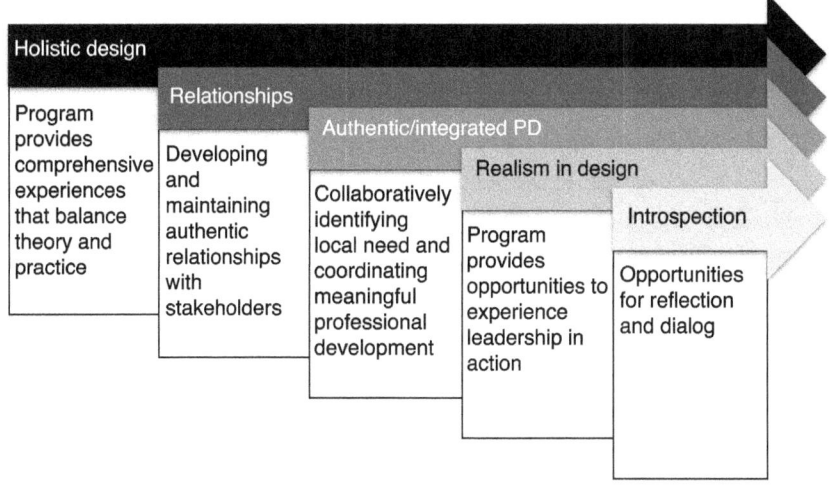

Figure 9.3 Holistic Leadership Development Design Model
Source: Author

Informal Gatherings

Providing opportunities for community is important. Role-alike communal gatherings (principals in one group, assistant principals in another) are important for developing professional networks. Informal opportunities to gather provide a unique chance for leaders to discuss their work and experiences in a less intense setting than their daily practice. Often, because of the demands of the job, administrators do not set aside time for informal connections with colleagues. Leadership Development Systems can carve out protected time where role-alike leaders are engaged in conversations around practice in a more informal setting. These informal gatherings should not be a required part of the system, meaning the leaders should not be mandated to attend. Once a mandate is attached to an activity, the tone and tenor of the event change. If possible, funding should be set aside as an incentive to fund informal gathering opportunities that would otherwise cost the administrator. Below are examples of informal gathering opportunities that can be constructed and organized in a Leadership Development System. It is ideal that one lead role-alike administrator coordinate the informal gatherings, rather than a person who is in charge of the overall system. For example, a lead principal can coordinate a coffee gathering for her or his colleagues, rather than the principal supervisor.

Coffee Gatherings

A lead role-alike administrator can coordinate opportunities for leaders to connect over coffee prior to the start of the work day. Informal chances like this to socialize can help form strong professional bonds between colleagues.

Morning Walks

A different approach to connecting in the morning comprises morning walks (or hikes in the case of the Learner-Centered Leadership program). For example, the Learner-Centered Leadership program used mountain hikes as part of their leadership development opportunities. Interested members of the initiative had the option to meet at a pre-designated hiking area and hike for two hours, followed by breakfast. This is a different approach to team building outside of the traditional work structure.

Sunrise Storytelling

Administrators have incredibly busy days. Often by the time the school day ends, an administrator still has several hours of work to do before being able to leave. Informal opportunities to gather before the school day begins allow administrators to meet with colleagues at a time when they are refreshed and better able to focus on their own work, rather than getting together after work when they are tired and focused on the events of the day.

Sunrise Storytelling begins prior to the workday at a location convenient to the group. This can be a local park, a library, a mall, or some other non-work location. In the Learning-Centered Leadership Project in Arizona, district administrators from Alhambra and Creighton convened in an early morning setting to commune over coffee and stories. These stories were entertaining ones around their teaching practices and leadership experiences. In this way, the administrators were able to craft a sense of community and connect in a way that was unavailable to them in more formal administrative settings (Danzig & Klitz, 2014).

Intensive Development Opportunities

There are a variety of possibilities for engaging in intensive development opportunities with aspiring and current school leaders. Ultimately, the design and format are determined by the needs analysis, the capacity of the organization and partners to implement development sessions, and the scheduled availability of participants. Any leadership development initiative must be sustained and long-term in order to be effective and have a lasting impact. However, this does not mean that initiatives cannot include periods of intense development that involve a condensed schedule. Three types of intensive opportunities are described below and can be modified to meet the specific needs of the system in which they are being implemented.

Retreat—Retreats tend to be single-day or two-day opportunities to leave the current workplace and engage in deep and critical explorations of specific leadership topics. While ideally implemented outside of the educational organization, retreats can be hosted within an organization facility based upon the fiscal constraints of the organization. Retreats are generally intensive sessions that involve the cohort members of the initiative and those implementing the development activities without interruption from outside factors, including work from the educational organization.

Institute—An institute generally involves two to three days of focus on a specific theme with breakout/sub-themes related to the topic of the institute. The same level of intensity as a retreat applies with institutes, and they can be held either off-site or on-site within the educational organization, again that being determined by fiscal availability. Institutes tend to be contained within the same cohort, like retreats.

Conference—Conferences involve more than a single cohort of school leaders. In fact, conferences can involve both aspiring and current school leaders. Conference length can vary from a single day to a week-long event, depending on the scope, focus, and number of participants. Conference design can take on many different shapes and formats. Designers should not be constrained to a singular design model when considering the conference format. The use of design teams—a group with representative members drawn from potential conference participants—led by a conference facilitator will help to craft a conference that meets the various development needs of the attendees. It is recommended that any conference design process begin at least nine months prior to the conference to provide enough lead time for development.

Figure 9.4 shows one way to conceptualize the integration of these development opportunities within a framework for supporting new leaders.

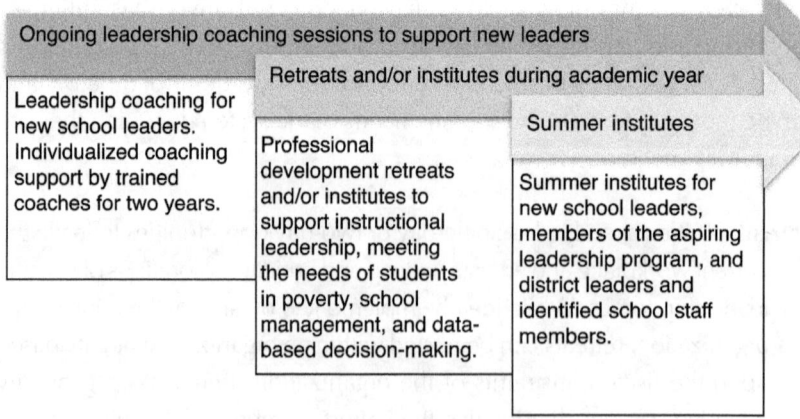

Figure 9.4 Integrated Leadership Development Model Example

Source: Author

Leadership Development Model

Dr. Leslie Hazle Bussey, Chief of Staff for the Georgia Leadership Institute for School Improvement (GLISI), shares more below about GLISI's Leadership Development Model.

The Georgia Leadership Institute for School Improvement (GLISI, http://glisi.org) "is an independent, non-profit organization that is committed to working with district and school leaders to build leadership capacity, improve organizational effectiveness, and create conditions that improve student achievement. We partner with education leaders in Georgia and across the nation to drive positive change in their districts and schools through performance-based leadership development, district consulting, and research, drawing on best practice in K-12 education, business, and adult learning." GLISI's approach to developing leaders along a continuum is outlined below.

School leaders, no matter how talented and well trained, cannot sustain transformative change alone. In the most successful schools, principals activate teacher leaders to advance change through their daily classroom practice and through collaboration with others (Spillane, Halverson, & Diamond, 2001). District leaders also have an impact on the conditions in which principals work, and therefore on how effective principals can be in leading and sustaining change (Burkhauser et al., 2013). GLISI's teacher and leader development model has three components:

- Leadership Learning Communities
- Individualized On-Site Coaching
- Central Office Transformation.

Leadership Learning Communities

Teams comprised of principals, assistant principals, and teachers learn essential leadership skills and begin using those skills together to address an authentic problem of practice in their school with guidance from skilled facilitators. Our research-based curriculum is focused on transforming culture, analyzing data and student work, and making high-impact adjustments to instruction and student support in order to improve performance.

Individualized On-Site Coaching

Experienced coaches provide on-site observation and feedback to leadership teams as they begin to practice and refine their skills in addressing their problem of practice. This is the heart of the process by which individual leaders develop expert skill through a cycle of authentic practice and frequent feedback.

Central Office Transformation

Without day to day expectations and support for superior leadership practice in schools, school teams are unlikely to sustain change. GLISI provides technical assistance and executive coaching for central office to build infrastructure and capacity in district leaders in leader selection, hiring, evaluation and growth of leaders informed by emerging research on central office transformation.

There are five steps to begin this work with a district partner:

1. District leaders express interest and commitment to growing teachers and leaders in partnership with GLISI.
2. GLISI conducts a readiness assessment to determine if key conditions for success are present.
3. Initiative launch takes place to engage school-based leaders in design of work toward performance goals.
4. Selection process is implemented in collaboration with principals, including assessment of teacher dispositions and leadership readiness/promise.
5. Monthly learning community/coaching/central office technical assistance, being scaffolded by strong project management and evaluation to ensure frequent and effective communication between GLISI and district partner.

Leadership Development Needs Assessment Tool

The Leadership Development Needs Assessment provides a baseline picture of leadership development within an organization. The following provides a starting point from which to assess needs. Individual organizations should add additional components as needed.

Leadership Role Inventory:
(Identify each leadership role, both formal and informal)
> Leadership Role Title
> Leadership Role Summary
> Essential Duties

Include as many roles as possible, but also allow space in your assessment for staff to include other roles that the organization may not be aware of such as a specific teach leader position and a leadership team role at a school site.

Current Leadership Development Partners:

(Is there a current Memorandum of Understanding?)

Collect all active memorandum of understandings (formal and informal) in order to understand in aggregate the various professional agreements with other institutions. Current grant initiatives should be included in this as they generally outline partner responsibilities as well. In addition, contracts with partners should be included that outline partner responsibilities.

Potential Leadership Development Partners:

Brainstorm potential leadership development partners. Inclusion of stakeholder voice in this process is important, as external stakeholders may be aware of additional potential partners that can bring a value-added component to the organization.

Current Leadership Development Initiatives:

All departments within a district at the central office should be surveyed, as a part of this needs assessment. Every development initiative, even tangentially connected to leadership development, needs to be identified. These initiatives can then be better understood by the needs assessment committee. Overlapping initiatives can be targeted to better utilize resources, interconnected initiatives can be identified, and conflicting initiatives can be highlighted to be addressed.

Previous Leadership Development Initiatives (previous ten years):

Previous development initiatives have an impact on new and future activities. A historical view of past development activities can help in crafting new initiatives in the future.

Anticipated Future Leadership Development Needs:

While requiring a bit of forecasting for the future and perhaps not always hitting the target directly, this list of anticipated needs can help plan for the future and aid the adaptive nature of the system. This list should involve both realistic possibilities, as well as possibilities that may be a bit more far-reaching in scope. It is easier to prepare for the future if all possibilities are explored. Again, the voice and viewpoint of multiple stakeholders are important in this process in order to get the best picture possible for the future.

Description of the Current Leadership Development System:

Multiple stakeholders—central office, building level, and external partners—need to participate in the description process. Generally this can be done by:

- *gathering evidence and materials of the current system*
- *seeking out individual feedback on the system by multiple stakeholders*
- *using focus groups to learn about the system*

It is typically easier for the person or department not coordinating the current Leadership Development System to conduct this description process. An individual or department less connected to the system will have a less biased approach to the process.

Resources Available:

Cycling resources is important in an ecological approach to leadership development. The first step is to identify all resources available for the system. These include fiscal resource, human capital, existing infrastructure, and partner resources. Again, involving multiple viewpoints in the process is helpful as there may be resources available that are not currently being utilized by the system or can be used in the future.

The Learning-Centered Leadership Development Program

Jianping Shen, Professor of Educational Leadership, Research and Technology at Western Michigan University, shares his thoughts about the

Learning-Centered Leadership Development Program through his university, as well as a variety of tools available to districts for integration into a Leadership Development System.

With the support of a five-year grant from the School Leadership Program of the US Department of Education, Jianping Shen and his colleagues developed a Learning-Centered Leadership Development Program for Practicing and Aspiring Principals. The program focuses on both the content and the process of the school improvement process. In terms of content, the program focuses on seven dimensions of school leadership associated with student learning: (a) commitment and passion for school renewal, (b) orderly school operation, (c) high, cohesive, and culturally relevant expectations for all students, (d) coherent curricular programs, (e) distributive and empowering leadership, (f) real-time and embedded instructional assessment, and (g) data-informed decision making. In terms of process, the program focuses on the five levels of learning outlined by Marzano and his colleagues: from (a) *experiential*, to (b) *declarative*, (c) *procedural*, (d) *contextual*, and (e) *evidential*. The program engages participants in using a renewal model, rather than the typical reform model.

- For more details about the program, see: Shen, J. & Cooley, V. E. (2012). Learning-centered leadership development program for practicing and aspiring principals. In K. L. Sanzo, S. Myran, and A. H. Normore (Eds.), *Successful school leadership preparation and development: Lessons learned from US DoE School Leadership Program grants* (pp. 113–135). Bingley, United Kingdom: Emerald Group Publishing.
- For a description of the research, best practice, and tools for the seven dimensions of school leadership, see: Shen, J. & Cooley, V. E. (Eds.) (2013). *A resource book for improving principals' learning-centered leadership*. New York, NY: Peter Lang Publishing.
- For case studies on how school leadership teams engage in school renewal to improve student achievement, and for the evaluative results on the positive effect of the Learning-Centered Leadership Development Program on principal leadership and student achievement, see: Shen, J. & Burt, W. (Eds.) (in press). *Learning-centered school leadership: School renewal in action*. New York, NY: Peter Lang Publishing. It includes case studies on how school leadership teams engage in school renewal to improve student achievement. The case studies, co-authored by

university personnel and school personnel, show real-life school improvement work.

- For a discussion of the sustainability of the renewal activities and the renewal model for the Learning-Centered Leadership Development Program, see: (a) Burt, W., Shen, J., Leneway, R., & Rainey, M. (2014). Sustaining data-informed decision-making. In K. L. Sanzo (Ed.), *From policy to practice: Sustaining innovations in school leadership preparation and development* (pp. 101–120). Charlotte, NC: Information Age Publishing; and (b) Reeves, P., Palmer, L. B., McCrumb, D., & Shen, J. (2014). Sustaining a renewal model for school improvement. In K. L. Sanzo (Ed.), *From policy to practice: Sustaining innovations in school leadership preparation and development* (pp. 267–292). Charlotte, NC: Information Age Publishing.

Model Teacher Program

Developing and Refining Employee Expertise

Angela Rhett, Program Administrator for Employee Expertise in Newport News Public Schools in Virginia, shares their approach to crafting a model to support expert teacher leader development. For more information contact: angela.rhett@nn.k12.va.us.

Every school division has exemplary teachers who are models of excellence in the field. High-performing teachers have much to offer beyond the four walls of their classrooms. These educators are trailblazers in the profession who seek and demand the best from themselves and their students. Colleagues can learn much from collaborating with their high-caliber peers; however, leaders must remain mindful that our best teachers also need an opportunity to refine and expand their skill sets. While many professional development efforts are focused on improving the performance of mediocre to proficient teachers, the model teacher program in Newport News Public Schools is designed with a multi-faceted purpose. This program supports teacher development across ability levels and cultivates leadership skills among a promising pool of talented educators.

Curriculum supervisors, who have in-depth knowledge of teaching and learning across the division, recommend exceptional educators to serve as model teachers for the upcoming school year. Model teachers offer support

Adding to Your Leadership Development Toolkit

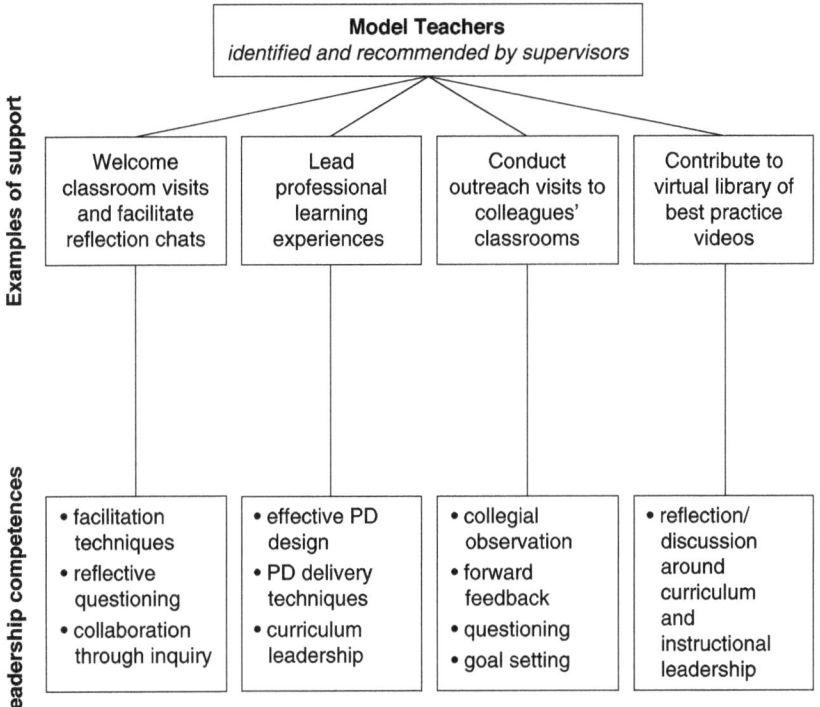

Figure 9.5 Model Teacher Program Framework
Source: © Angela Rhett. Used with permission.

to their colleagues in a variety of ways (see Figure 9.5). They welcome fellow teachers for classroom visits and offer follow-up reflection chats to debrief the observation, discuss strategies and considerations, and address existing questions. Model teachers collaborate with central office personnel to design and offer specialized professional development opportunities specifically for new teachers. This stretches model teachers and invites them to develop important skills related to the design and delivery of learning experiences steeped in the principles of adult learning theory. Model teachers also visit new teachers in their classrooms, offering feedback and support based on a focused target. This flipped scenario develops the hard and soft skills related to collegial observation and discussion. Finally, all teachers are able to virtually visit the model teachers' classrooms through a video series highlighting best practices in action. Videos are developed to showcase high-yield strategies that span content areas and levels.

The model teacher program has proven rewarding and successful. A cadre of empowered teachers has emerged. It is viewed as an honor to be part of the model teacher team, and the chosen teachers are eager to support their colleagues throughout the journey. Furthermore, model teachers are exploring and refining their leadership potential. Teachers who may not have realized their innate abilities have a chance to hone their skills as they learn with and from their colleagues. The mutual benefits of the model teacher program are unmistakable and inspiring.

Site Visits

Visiting school and other learning organization sites is a valuable strategy for leadership development. Often, school leaders have limited experience in terms of the number of school buildings and other learning organizations they have visited and engaged with in their work. Collaborative and intentionally structured visits with multiple school leaders and aspiring leaders can be an informative process. The following are three examples:

- *Learning Exchanges:* The Northeast Leadership Academy 2.0 proposed "Learning Exchanges" in the 2013 School Leadership Program funding proposal. Grant participants visit school sites that utilize robust technology for instruction.
- *Job Shadowing:* Assistant Principals and first year principals participate in peer leader shadowing opportunities. Leaders are assigned a partner within their cohort. Each leader will visit another school and host a visiting principal. This peer shadowing opportunity allows the leader to learn from another leader and also allows the leader to share the work with a colleague. A four square capture sheet is provided to assist leaders as they capture ideas and evidence of focus areas around: Data-Driven Instruction, Student Culture, Teacher Feedback, Professional Development, Staff Culture, Planning, and Leadership Team Development (shared by Sheila Armstrong and Debi Boyles, Principal Coaches, Tulsa Public Schools system).
- *Instructional Rounds*: The Leading to Learn program through the Green River Regional Educational Cooperative (GRREC) works with high-poverty districts in south central Kentucky. Through the Leading to Learn program, principals and assistant principals learn to lead school change through a variety of engaging professional development

initiatives as part of a Leadership Development System. During the instructional rounds component, school leaders are trained as peer observers and participate in half-day site visit observations of instruction and student learning. The site visits focus specifically around an identified problem of practice. The leaders then engage in structured dialogue using an affinity protocol to identify root causes of the problem and develop recommendations. GRREC incorporates the following philosophy into instructional rounds use: "Rounds emphasize learning to see, unlearning to judge, and focus on improving the practice of teaching and learning across an entire building. This represents a significant shift from behaviorally-focused walk-through instruments to an honest, school-wide observation of the instructional core" (GRREC, 2013, p. 20).

Tools for Data-Informed Decision Making

With the accumulation of large amounts of educational data, data-informed decision making has been proposed as an approach to improving education. However, there are few tools to help school practitioners to measure and facilitate the work on data-informed decision making. Jianping Shen and his colleagues have developed the following two tools.

Data-Informed Decision-Making on High-Impact Strategies: An Inventory for School Principals: This is a quantitative tool that measures the extent to which principals engage in data-informed decision making on high-impact strategies. By high-impact strategies, the authors mean the 11 factors that are associated with high student achievement that are identified in Marzano's book *What Works in Schools*: (a) guaranteed and viable curriculum, (b) challenging goals and effective feedback, (c) parent and community involvement, (d) safe and orderly environment, (e) collegiality and professionalism, (f) instructional strategies, (g) classroom management, (h) classroom curriculum design, (i) home environment, (j) learned intelligence, and (k) student motivation. The instrument could be used by both principals themselves for self-improvement and by teachers to rate their principals. It can be downloaded free from www.wmich.edu/wallacegrant/docs/DIDM-INST.pdf. For psychometric properties about the instrument, see the following three articles:

(a) Shen, J., Ma, X., Cooley, V. E. & Burt, W. L. (in press). Measuring principals' data-informed decision-making on high-impact strategies: Validating an instrument used by teachers. *Journal of School Leadership*;

(b) Shen, J., Ma, X., Cooley, V. E. & Burt, W. L. (in press). Mediating effects of school process on the relationship between principals' data-informed decision-making and student achievement. *International Journal of Leadership in Education*. DOI: 10.1080/13603124.2014.986208; and

(c) Shen, J., Cooley, V., Ma, X., Reeves, P., Burt, W., Rainey, J. M., & Yuan, W. (2012). Data-informed decision-making on high-impact strategies: Developing and validating an instrument for Principals. *Journal of Experimental Education, 80*(1), 1–25.

Data-Informed Decision-Making: A Guidebook of Data Points and Analyses in the Context of Michigan School Improvement Framework: This is a tool developed by a team of university faculty members and 16 principals from four school districts in Michigan. The Michigan School Improvement Framework is similar to other frameworks for school improvement. It has five strands: (a) teaching for learning, (b) leadership, (c) personal and professional development, (d) school and community relations, and (e) data and information management. Within each strand, there are also standards and benchmarks. For the first strand of "(a) teaching for learning," there are three strands: (a1) curriculum, (a2) instruction, and (a3) assessment. For "(a1) curriculum," there are two benchmarks: (a1A) curriculum aligned, reviewed, and monitored, and (a1B) curriculum communicated. All together the framework has 5 strands, 13 standards, and 26 benchmarks. The guidebook proposes two specific data points and data analysis approaches for each benchmark.

This guidebook was developed to address the data needs embedded in the school improvement process. Authors take the strands, standards, and benchmarks from the framework, and develop two examples of data point and data analysis for each benchmark. The importance of data-informed decision making is self-evident. The guidebook is intended to provide concrete examples for educators.

The document has the following characteristics to meet the needs from the field:

1. More summative than formative. While the discussion questions in Michigan School Improvement Framework lead to more formative evaluation, the data source and the data analysis suggested in the guidebook are more summative.
2. Decision-oriented. The examples of data points and data analyses are decision-oriented. A decision could be made after each data analysis.
3. Need-based. In a continuum from (a) an open-ended toolkit, to (b) an inquiry process and (c) a model of data points and analyses, the authors choose to focus on (c) because it is important to provide concrete examples for principals and other school personnel. The approach that authors chose to take addresses an urgent need in the field.
4. Catering to a wide range of audiences. The document is intended for educators in various capacities. This document could also be used as a curriculum guide on data-informed decision making by universities' educational leadership programs and professional associations' professional development. The guidebook can be downloaded free from www.wmich.edu/wallacegrant/docs/DIDM.pdf.

See the following chapter for more information about the guidebook: Shen, J., Cooley, V. E., Marx, G., Kirby, E., & Whale, D. E. (2012). Data-informed decision-making: A guidebook for data points and analyses for the school improvement team. In J. Shen (Ed.), *Tools for improving school principals' work* (pp. 137–168). New York: Peter Lang.

Tools for Improving Principals' Work

The vital role of the principal in improving schools in general and enhancing student achievement in particular has been well documented. Given its importance, there is a need to improve the role of the principal, particularly in those dimensions associated with student achievement. In light of the accountability movement, with its particular focus on student achievement, and the advent of the evaluation era (including the evaluation of principals), the need for tools is even more urgent. The edited volume below presents those tools with the aim of improving learning-centered principalship and is useful for principals and others.

Shen, J. (Ed.) (2012). *Tools for improving school principals' work*. New York: Peter Lang Publishing. The book includes information on recent tools on instructional leadership, including:

Vanderbilt Assessment of Leadership in Education (Val-Ed) by Andrew Porter et al.

Principal Instructional Management Rating Scale (PIMRS) by Philip Hallinger

The Organization of the School and Teacher Satisfaction with Their Work Environment by Ronald Heck and George Marcoulides

Data-Informed Decision-Making on High-Impact Strategies: An Inventory for School Principals by Jianping Shen et al.

Data-Informed Decision-Making: A Guidebook of Data Points and Analyses in the Context of Michigan School Improvement Framework by Jianping Shen et al.

The Leadership Performance Planning Worksheet (LPPW) by Lynn M. Scott

The SAM Process (with Time/Task Analysis™ and TimeTrack™)

High Schools That Work School Improvement Model by James E. Bottoms and Paula Egelson.

Transition Plan for Systems

Often the creation (or redesign) of a new initiative in an organization is infused with some fiscal resources that are not always sustainable. However, the initiative being created is usually coupled with an expectation that the initiative be sustainable past the life of extra funds. It is imperative, therefore, to "begin with the end in mind" and craft a plan for implementation which takes into account the potential final budget compared to the initial budget, which identifies effective program features and sustainable aspects of those features that can be implemented without additional funds, and which crafts a plan for sustainability. Figure 9.6 shows a model the design team can reflect upon throughout the development and implementation of the initial phases of the new (or redesigned) Leadership Development System.

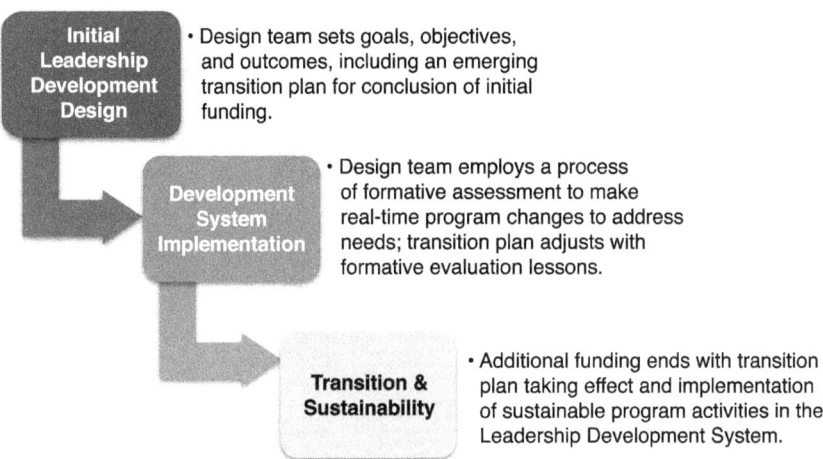

Figure 9.6 Leadership Development Program Sustainability Model
Source: Author

References

Allen, K. E., Stelzner, S. P., & Wielkiewicz, R. M. (1998). The ecology of leadership: Adapting to the challenges of a changing world. *Journal of Leadership Studies, 5*(2), 62–82.

Augustine, C. H., Gonzalez, G., Ikemoto, G. S., Russell, J., Zellman, G. L., Constant, L., Armstrong, J., & Dembosky, J. W. (2009). *Improving school leadership: The promise of cohesive leadership systems*. Santa Monica, CA: RAND Corporation.

Barnett, B. G., Basom, M. R., Yerkes, D. M., & Norris, C. J. (2000). Cohorts in educational leadership programs: Benefits, difficulties, and the potential for developing school leaders. *Educational Administration Quarterly, 36*(2), 255–282.

Bastian, K. C. & Henry, G. T. (2014, December). The apprentice: Pathways to the principalship and student achievement. *Educational Administration Quarterly*, 1–40.

Bellamy, G. T., Crockett, J. B., & Nordengren, C. (2014). *Preparing school leaders for every student's learning*. CEEDAR Document No. LS-2. Washington, DC: Office of Special Education Programs, US Department of Education.

Belle, D. & Sanzo, K. (2014). The experiences of women in a U.S. Department of Education school leadership preparation cohort program. In K. L. Sanzo (Ed.), *From policy to practice: Sustainable innovations in school leadership preparation and development*. (pp. 213–236). Charlotte, NC: Information Age Publishing.

Beteille, T., Kalogrides, D., & Loeb, S. (2012). Stepping stones: Principal career paths and school outcomes. *Social Science Research, 41*(4), 904–919.

References

Bloom, G., Castagna, C., Moir, E., & Warren, B. (2005). *Blended coaching: Skills and strategies to support principal development.* Thousand Oaks, CA: Corwin Press.

Browne-Ferrigno, T. (2007). Developing school leaders: Practitioner growth during an advanced leadership development program for principals and administrator-trained teachers. *Journal of Research on Leadership Education, 2*(3), 1–30. Available at www.ucea.org/.

Browne-Ferrigno, T. (2014). Preparing principals for high-need rural schools. In K. L. Sanzo (Ed.), *From policy to practice: Sustainable innovations in school leadership preparation and development* (pp. 23–46). Charlotte, NC: Information Age Publishing.

Browne-Ferrigno, T. & Muth, R. (2006). Leadership mentoring and situated learning: Catalysts for principalship readiness and lifelong mentoring. *Mentoring & Tutoring, 14*(3), 275–295.

Browne-Ferrigno, T., & Muth, R. (2008). Recruitment and retention of quality principals: Essential for successful schools. *CAPEA Educational Leadership and Administration: Teaching and Program Development, 20*, 19–45.

Burke, W., Marx, G. E., & Lowenstein, E. (2012). Leading, leadership, and learning: Exploring new contexts for leadership development in emerging school environments. *Planning and Changing, 43*(1/2), 113–126.

Burkhauser, S., Gates, S., Hamilton, L., Li, J., & Pierson, A. (2013). *Laying the foundation for successful school leadership.* RAND corporation research report. Los Angeles, CA: RAND Corporation.

Burt, W., Shen, J., Leneway, R., & Rainey, M. (2014). Sustaining data-informed decision-making. In K. L. Sanzo (Ed.), *From policy to practice: Sustaining innovations in school leadership preparation and development* (pp. 101–120). Charlotte, NC: Information Age Publishing.

Bush Institute. (2015). *Gwinnett county public schools: A systemic approach to scaling effective school leadership.*

Castetter, W. B. & Young, I. P. (2000). *The human resource function in educational administration (7th edition).* Upper Saddle River, NJ: Merrill/Prentice Hall.

Corcoran, S. P., Schwartz, A. E., & Weinstein, M. (2012). Training your own: The impact of New York City's aspiring principals program on

References

student achievement. *Educational Evaluation and Policy Analysis, 34*(2), 232–253.

Danzig, A. & Kiltz, G. (2014). Reflections on what was learned in the US department of education funded learner-centered leadership (LCL) project 2002–2006. In K. L. Sanzo (Ed.), *From policy to practice: Sustainable innovations in school leadership preparation and development* (pp.71–100). Charlotte, NC: Information Age Publishing.

Daresh, J. (2004). Mentoring school leaders: Professional promise or predictable problems? *Educational Administrative Quarterly, 40*(495), 495–517.

Darling-Hammond, L. (2010). *The flat world of education: How America's commitment to equity will determine our future.* New York: Teachers College Press.

Darling-Hammond, L., Meyerson, D., LaPointe, M., & Orr, M. (2009). *Preparing principals for a changing world: Lessons from effective school leadership programs.* San Francisco, CA: Jossey Bass.

Davis, J. & Wilson, S. M. (2000). Principal's efforts to empower teachers: Effects on teacher motivation and job satisfaction and stress. *Clearing House, 73*, 349–353.

Davis, S., Darling-Hammond, L., LaPointe, M., & Meyerson, D. (2005). *School leadership study: Developing successful principals.* Retrieved from Wallace Foundation website: www.wallacefoundation.org/knowledge-center/school-leadership/principal-training/Documents/Developing-Successful-Principals.pdf.

Davis, S. H., Leon, R. J., & Fultz, M. L. (2012). The power of institutional partnership in the development of turn around school leaders. In K. L. Sanzo, S. Myran, A. H. Normore (Eds.), *Successful school leadership preparation and development* (Advances in Educational Administration, Volume 17) (pp. 25–48). Bingley, United Kingdom: Emerald Group Publishing Limited.

Dufour, R. & Eaker, R. (1998). *Professional learning communities at work: Best practices for enhancing student achievement.* Bloomington, IN: Solution Tree.

Duncan, H. E. & Stock, M. J. (2010). Mentoring and coaching rural school leaders: What do they need? *Mentoring & Tutoring: Partnership in Learning, 18*(3), 293–311.

Eraut, M. (1994). *Developing professional knowledge and competence*. London: Falmer Press.

Folke, C., Hahn, T., Olsson, P., & Norberg, J. (2005). Adaptive governance of social-ecological systems. *Annual Review of Environment and Resources, 30*, 441–473.

Fullan, M. (2005). *Leadership and sustainability: System thinkers in action*. Thousand Oaks, CA: Corwin Press.

Fullan, M. & Knight, J. (2011). Coaches as system leaders. *Educational Leadership, 69*(2), 50–53.

Goddard, Y. L., Goddard, R. D., & Tschannen-Moran, M. (2007). A theoretical and empirical investigation of teacher collaboration for school improvement and student achievement in public elementary schools. *Teachers College Record, 109*(4), 877–896.

Green River Regional Educational Cooperative (GRREC). (2013). *Leading to learn*. US Department of Education School Leadership Program Application.

Grissom, J. & Loeb, S. (2011). Triangulating principal effectiveness: How perspectives of parents, teachers, and assistant principals identify the central importance of managerial skills. *American Educational Research Journal, 48*, 2091–2123.

Hale, E. L. & Moorman, H. N. (2003). *Preparing school principals: A national perspective on policy and program innovations*. Washington, DC: Institute for Educational Leadership.

Hattie, J. (2009). *A synthesis of over 800 meta-analyses relating to achievement*. New York: Routledge.

Heifetz, R., Grashow, A., & Linksy, M. (2009). *The practice of adaptive leadership: Tools and tactics for changing your organization and the world*. Boston, MA: Cambridge Leadership Associates.

Hopkins-Thompson, P. A. (2000). Colleagues helping colleagues: Mentoring and coaching. *NASSP: Leading Schools, 84*(29), 29–36.

Innes, J. & Booher, D. (2003). The impact of collaborative planning on governance capacity. *IURD Working Paper Series*. Institute of Urban and Regional Development. Retrieved September 19, 2011, from http://repositories.cdlib.org/iurd/wps/WP-2003-03.

Issa Lahera, A. & Normore, A. (2014). Sustaining school leadership programs: Planning for leadership succession, recruitment, selection, and

References

innovative curriculum. In K. L. Sanzo (Ed.), *From policy to practice: Sustainable innovations in preparation and development* (pp. 1–22). Charlotte, NC: Information Age Publishing.

Jackson, B. L. & Kelly, C. (2002). Exceptional and innovative programs in educational leadership. *Educational Administration Quarterly, 38*(2), 192–212.

King, C. L. (2014). *Quality Measures Partnership Effectiveness Continuum*. Waltham, MA: Education Development Center, Inc.

Lave, J. & Wenger, E. (1991). *Situated learning: Legitimate peripheral participation*. Cambridge, MA: Cambridge University Press.

Leithwood, K., Seashore Louis, K., Anderson, S., & Wahlstrom, K. (2004). *Review of research: How leadership influences student learning*. New York: Wallace Foundation.

Levine, A. (2005). *Educating school leaders*. Princeton, NJ: The Education Schools Project.

Lochmiller, C. R. & Silver, M. (2010). Accelerating new principal development through leadership coaching. In A. Shoho, B. Barnett, & A. K. Tooms, *The challenges for new principals in the twenty-first century*. Charlotte, NC: Information Age Publishing.

Lovely, S. (2004). *Staffing the principalship: Finding, coaching, and mentoring school leaders*. Alexandria, VA: ASCD.

Lutz, F. W. & Ferrante, R. (1972). *Emergent practices in the continuing education of school administrators*. Columbus, OH: University Council for Educational Administration.

Marzano, R. J. (2003). *What works in schools*. Alexandria, VA: ASCD.

Mast, J., Scribner, J., & Sanzo, K. (2011). Authentic planning for leadership preparation and development. *Educational Planning, 20*(2).

Miller, P. & Hafner, M. (2008). Moving toward dialogical collaboration: A critical examination of a university–school–community partnership. *Educational Administration Quarterly, 44*(1), 66–110.

Murphy, J. (2005). Unpacking the foundations of ISLLC standards and addressing concerns in the academic community. *Educational Administration Quarterly, 41*(1), 154–191.

Murphy, J. & Vriesenga, M. (2006). Research on school leadership preparation in the United States: An analysis. *School Leadership and Management, 26*(2), 183–195.

References

Myran, S., Crum, K. S., & Clayton, K. (2010). Four pillars of effective university-school district partnerships: Implications for educational planning. *Educational Planning, 19*(2), 46–60.

Newman, F. & Associates. (1996). *School restructuring and authentic student achievement*. San Francisco, CA: Jossey Bass.

Normore, A. H. (2004). Recruitment and selection: Meeting the leadership shortage in one large Canadian school district. *Canadian Journal of Educational Administration and Policy, 30*, 1–15. Retrieved from www.umanitoba.ca/publications/cjeap/.

Northeast Leadership Academy 2.0. (2013). *The northeast leadership academy 2.0: Developing and sustaining effective leaders for high-need rural schools*. US Department of Education School Leadership Proposal.

Orr, M. T. (2006). Educating leaders for tomorrow: Mapping innovation in leadership preparation in our nation's schools of education. *Phi Delta Kappan, 87*(7), 492–499.

Reeves, P., Palmer, L. B., McCrumb, D., & Shen, J. (2014). Sustaining a renewal model for school improvement. In K. L. Sanzo (Ed.), *From policy to practice: Sustaining innovations in school leadership preparation and development* (pp. 267–292). Charlotte, NC: Information Age Publishing.

Riley, P. (2009). The development and testing of a time-limited mentoring model for experienced school leaders. *Mentoring & Tutoring: Partnership in Learning, 17*(3), 233–249.

Roberts, A. (2000). Mentoring revisited: A phenomenological reading of the literature. *Mentoring & Tutoring, 8*(2), 145–170.

Robertson, J. (2005). *Coaching leadership: Building educational leadership capacity through coaching partnerships*. Wellington, New Zealand: NZCER Press.

Robinson, V., Lloyd, C., & Rowe, K. (2008). The impact of leadership on student outcomes: An analysis of the differential effectives of leadership types. *Educational Administration Quarterly, 44*, 635–674.

Rodriguez-Campos, L., Rincones-Gomez, R., & Shen, J. (2005). Secondary principals' educational attainment, experience, and professional development in the USA. *International Journal of Leadership in Education, 8*(4), 309–319.

Rosenholtz, S. J. (1991). *Teachers' workplace: The social organization of schools*. New York: Teachers College Press.

References

Salter, T. (2008). Exploring current thinking within the field of coaching on the role of supervision. *International Journal of Evidence Based Coaching and Mentoring, 2*, 27–39.

Sanzo, K. L., Myran, S., & Caggiano, J. (2015). *Formative assessment leadership: Identify, plan, apply, assess, and refine*. New York: Routledge.

Scribner, J. P., Cockrell, K. S., Cockrell, D. H., & Valentine, J. W. (1999). Creating professional communities in schools through organizational learning: An evaluation of a school improvement process. *Educational Administration Quarterly, 2*(1), 130–160.

Seashore Louis, K. S., Marks, H. M., & Kruse, S. (1996). Teachers' professional community in restructuring schools. *American Educational Research Journal, 33*(4), 757–798.

Sharratt, L. & Fullan, M. (2009). Interdependent practice. In *Realization: The change imperative for deepening district-wide reform*. Thousand Oaks, CA: Corwin Press.

Shen, J. (Ed.) (2012). *Tools for improving school principals' work*. New York: Peter Lang Publishing.

Shen, J. & Burt, W. (Eds.) (in press). *Learning-centered school leadership: School renewal in action*. New York: Peter Lang Publishing.

Shen, J. & Cooley, V. E. (2012). Learning-centered leadership development program for practicing and aspiring principals. In K. L. Sanzo, S. Myran, & A. H. Normore (Eds.), *Successful school leadership preparation and development: Lessons learned from US DoE School Leadership Program grants* (pp. 113–135). UK: Emerald Group Publishing.

Shen, J. & Cooley, V. E. (Eds.) (2013). *A resource book for improving principals' learning-centered leadership*. New York: Peter Lang Publishing.

Shen, J., Cooley, V., Ma, X., Reeves, P., Burt, W., Rainey, J. M., & Yuan, W. (2012). Data-informed decision-making on high-impact strategies: Developing and validating an instrument for principals. *Journal of Experimental Education, 80*(1), 1–25.

Shen, J., Cooley, V. E., Marx, G., Kirby, E., & Whale, D. E. (2012). Data-informed decision-making: A guidebook for data points and analyses for the school improvement team. In J. Shen (Ed.), *Tools for improving school principals' work* (pp. 137–168). New York: Peter Lang.

Shen, J., Ma, X., Cooley, V. E. & Burt, W. L. (in press). Measuring principals' data-informed decision-making on high-impact strategies: Validating an instrument used by teachers. *Journal of School Leadership*.

Southern Regional Education Board. (2005). *The principal internship: How can we get it right?* Atlanta, GA: Southern Regional Education Board.

Spillane, J., Halverson, R., & Diamond, J. (2001). Investigating school leadership practice: A distributed perspective. *Educational Researcher, 30*(3), 23–28.

Steele, M. D., Johnson, K. R., Otten, S., Herbel-Eisenmann, B. A., & Carver, C. (2015). Improving instructional leadership through the development of leadership content knowledge: The case of principal learning in algebra. *Journal of Research on Leadership Education*. DOI: 10.1177/1942775115569353.

Stephens, J. P. & Boland, J. P. (2015). The aesthetic knowledge problem of problem-solving with design thinking. *Journal of Management Inquiry, 24*(3), 219–232.

Supovitz, J. (2014). *Building a lattice for school leadership: The top-to-bottom rethinking of leadership development in England and what it might mean for American education.* Research Report (#RR-83). Philadelphia, PA: Consortium for Policy Research in Education, University of Pennsylvania.

Supovitz, J. A. & Christman, J. B. (2003). Development communities of instructional practice: Lessons from Cincinnati and Philadelphia (CPRE Policy Briefs RB-39). Philadelphia: University of Pennsylvania, Graduate School of Education.

Tschannen-Moran, B. & Tschannen-Moran, M. (2010). *Evocative coaching: Transforming schools one conversation at a time.* San Francisco, CA: Jossey-Bass.

Turnbull, B. J., Riley, D., Arcaira, E., Anderson, L. M., & MacFarlane, J. R. (2013). *Building a stronger principalship, Volume 1: Six districts begin the principal pipeline initiative.* New York: Wallace Foundation.

US Department of Education, Office of Innovation and Improvement. (2004). *Innovations in education: Innovative pathways to school leadership.* Washington, DC.

Valdez, M., Broin, A., & Carroll, K. (2015). *Untapped: Transforming teacher leadership to help students succeed.* New York: New Leaders.

Wallace Foundation. (2013). *Districts matter: Cultivating the principals urban schools need.* New York.

References

Wallace Foundation. (n.d.). *The national SAM innovation project: Helping principals make time to focus on instructional leadership*. New York. www.wallacefoundation.org/Pages/SAM.aspx.

Wenger, E. (1998). *Communities of practice: Learning, meaning, and identity*. Cambridge University Press.

Western Michigan University. (2010). *Learning-centered leadership development program*. School Leadership Program Grant Application PR/Award #U363A100082. Kalamazoo, MI.

Whitaker, T. (2003). *What great teachers do differently: 14 things that matter most (1st edition)*. New York: Routledge.

Wielkiewicz, R. M. & Stelzner, S. P. (2005). An ecological perspective on leadership theory, research, and practice. *Review of General Psychology, 9*(4), 326–341.

Williams, E. J., Matthews, J., & Baugh, S. (2004). Developing a mentoring internship model for school leadership: Using legitimate peripheral participation. *Mentoring and Tutoring, 12*(1), 53–70.

Young, M. D., Petersen, G. J., & Short, P. M. (2002, April). The complexity of substantive reform: A call for interdependence among key stakeholders. *Educational Administrative Quarterly, 38*(2), 137–175.